Cambridge English

OFFICIAL PREPARATION MATERIAL

ADVANCED

CERTIFICATE IN ADVANCED ENGLISH

WITH ANSWERS

1

AUTHENTIC EXAMINATION PAPERS
FROM CAMBRIDGE ENGLISH
LANGUAGE ASSESSMENT

For revised exam from 2015

Cambridge University Press
www.cambridge.org/elt

Cambridge English Language Assessment
www.cambridgeenglish.org

Information on this title: www.cambridge.org/9781107653511

© Cambridge University Press and UCLES 2014

3rd printing 2015

Printed in Dubai by Oriental Press

A catalogue record of this book is available from the British Library

ISBN 978-1-107-65351-1 Student's Book with answers
ISBN 978-1-107-68958-9 Student's Book without answers
ISBN 978-1-107-66804-1 Audio CDs (2)
ISBN 978-1-107-65496-9 Student's Book Pack (Student's Book with answers and Audio CDs (2))

Contents

Introduction   *4*

Test 1   Reading and Use of English   *8*
Writing   *22*
Listening   *24*
Speaking   *29*

Test 2   Reading and Use of English   *30*
Writing   *44*
Listening   *46*
Speaking   *51*

Test 3   Reading and Use of English   *52*
Writing   *66*
Listening   *68*
Speaking   *73*

Test 4   Reading and Use of English   *74*
Writing   *88*
Listening   *90*
Speaking   *95*

Test 1   Frames for the Speaking test   *96*
Test 2   Frames for the Speaking test   *99*
Test 3   Frames for the Speaking test   *102*
Test 4   Frames for the Speaking test   *105*

Marks and results   *108*

Test 1   Key and transcript   *120*
Test 2   Key and transcript   *129*
Test 3   Key and transcript   *138*
Test 4   Key and transcript   *147*

Sample answer sheets   *156*

Thanks and acknowledgements   *167*

Visual materials for the Speaking test   *colour section*

Introduction

This collection of four complete practice tests comprises papers from the *Cambridge English: Advanced (CAE)*, examination; students can practise these tests on their own or with the help of a teacher.

The *Cambridge English: Advanced* examination is part of a suite of general English examinations produced by Cambridge English Language Assessment. This suite consists of five examinations that have similar characteristics but are designed for different levels of English language ability. Within the five levels, *Cambridge English: Advanced* is at Level C1 in the Council of Europe's *Common European Framework of Reference for Languages: Learning, teaching, assessment*.

It has been accredited by Ofqual, the statutory regulatory authority in England, at Level 2 in the National Qualifications Framework. The *Cambridge English: Advanced* examination is recognised by educational institutions, governmental departments and employers around the world as proof of the ability to follow an academic course of study in English at university level and communicate effectively at a managerial and professional level.

Examination	Council of Europe Framework Level	UK National Qualifications Framework Level
Cambridge English: Proficiency Certificate of Proficiency in English (CPE)	C2	3
Cambridge English: Advanced Certificate in Advanced English (CAE)	C1	2
Cambridge English: First First Certificate in English (FCE)	B2	1
Cambridge English: Preliminary Preliminary English Test (PET)	B1	Entry 3
Cambridge English: Key Key English Test (KET)	A2	Entry 2

Further information

The information contained in this practice book is designed to be an overview of the exam. For a full description of all of the above exams, including information about task types, testing focus and preparation, please see the relevant handbooks which can be obtained from Cambridge English Language Assessment at the address below or from the website at: www.cambridgeenglish.org

Cambridge English Language Assessment	Telephone: +44 1223 553997
1 Hills Road	Fax: +44 1223 553621
Cambridge CB1 2EU	email: helpdesk@cambridgeenglish.org
United Kingdom	

The structure of *Cambridge English: Advanced* – an overview

The *Cambridge English: Advanced* examination consists of four papers.

Reading and Use of English   1 hour 30 minutes
This paper consists of **eight** parts, with 56 questions. For Parts 1 to 4, the test contains texts with accompanying grammar and vocabulary tasks, and separate items with a grammar and vocabulary focus. For Parts 5 to 8, the test contains a range of texts and accompanying reading comprehension tasks.

Writing   1 hour 30 minutes
This paper consists of **two** parts which carry equal marks. In Part 1, which is **compulsory**, candidates must write an essay with a discursive focus of between 220 and 260 words. The task requires candidates to write an essay based on two points given in the input text. They need to explain which of the two points is more important and give reasons for their choice.

In Part 2, there are **three** tasks from which candidates **choose one** to write about. The tasks include a letter, a proposal, a report and a review. Candidates write between 220 and 260 words in this part.

Listening   40 minutes (approximately)
This paper consists of **four** parts with 30 questions. Each part contains a recorded text or texts and corresponding comprehension tasks. Each part is heard twice.

Speaking   15 minutes
The Speaking test consists of **four** parts. The standard test format is two candidates and two examiners. One examiner acts as both interlocutor and assessor and manages the interaction either by asking questions or providing cues for the candidates. The other acts as assessor and does not join in the conversation. The test consists of short exchanges with the interlocutor and with the other candidate, an individual long turn, a collaborative task involving both candidates, and a discussion.

Grading

The overall *Cambridge English: Advanced* grade is based on the total score gained in all four papers. All candidates receive a Statement of Results which includes a graphical profile of their performance in each of the four skills and Use of English. Certificates are given to candidates who pass the examination with grade A, B or C. Candidates who achieve grade A will receive the *Cambridge English: Advanced* certificate stating they have demonstrated ability at C2 level. Candidates whose performance is below C1 level, but falls within Level B2, receive a Cambridge English certificate stating they have demonstrated ability at B2 level. Candidates whose performance falls below Level B2 do not receive a certificate.

For further information on grading and results, go to the website (see page 5).

Test 1

READING AND USE OF ENGLISH (1 hour 30 minutes)

Part 1

For questions **1–8**, read the text below and decide which answer (**A**, **B**, **C** or **D**) best fits each gap. There is an example at the beginning (**0**).
Mark your answers **on the separate answer sheet**.

Example:

0 A esteemed   **B** viewed   **C** regarded   **D** believed

0	A	B	C	D
	☐	☐	☐	■

The camera never lies

Arthur Conan Doyle, creator of the Sherlock Holmes stories, **(0)** …….. himself to be a rational man, a scientist even. But in 1920, when he saw photographs of fairies taken in a garden **(1)** …..…. , he thought he was seeing scientific proof that these tiny creatures really existed. He published the photographs alongside an article he wrote, **(2)** …..…. fairies as supernatural wonders. It was not until 1939 that the two ladies who took the photos admitted these were **(3)** …..…. They simply cut out pictures of fairies from a book and **(4)** …..…. them among flowers. The results are **(5)** …..…. beautiful. But the simplicity of the trick **(6)** …..…. a basic principle of photography, that the camera cannot lie.

But it can, and always could. Today, we are used to computer software **(7)** …..…. us to rework our digital images and it is a **(8)** …..…. that photography ever had a true age of innocence. From the moment cameras began capturing reality, that reality was being altered.

1	A venue	B setting	C background	D surrounding
2	A calling	B naming	C attributing	D acknowledging
3	A false	B faulty	C fake	D fictional
4	A arranged	B spaced	C settled	D distributed
5	A categorically	B unavoidably	C substantially	D undeniably
6	A weakens	B undermines	C demolishes	D dismantles
7	A letting	B supporting	C enabling	D empowering
8	A fantasy	B legend	C dream	D myth

[Handwritten annotations]

concert

word grammar
as
calling sbdy X
naming " "

Meaning.
religon L1 / translation

fake – deliberately created to look like real

settle

√ H/W
Ans

Part 2

For questions **9–16**, read the text below and think of the word which best fits each gap. Use only **one** word in each gap. There is an example at the beginning (**0**).

Write your answers **IN CAPITAL LETTERS on the separate answer sheet**.

Example:

0	I	T																	

Online passwords – what everyone should know

When (**0**) …….. comes to online security, we all know what we ought to do: choose a different, random set of letters and numbers for every email account, shopping site or bank account. But hardly (**9**) ……. *anyone* does this, because memorising them all is impossible. So we use the same familiar words for every site, (**10**) ……. *like* a pet's name or, even worse, the word 'password', occasionally remembering to replace the letter O with a zero, or choosing to (**11**) …….. *make* use of a capital letter.

Even if we opt (**12**) …….. *to* a random group of letters such as 'fpqzy', there is now software available which can make a thousand guesses per second, enabling a hacker to get to your password in just under four hours.

Interestingly, (**13**) …….. *when* increasing your password to twenty random letters, you increase a hacker's guessing time to 6.5 thousand trillion centuries. The problem is that you would (**14**) …….. *have* no chance of ever remembering those 20 letters. The solution, apparently, is to come (**15**) …*up*… with three or four short, unrelated words and work (**16**) …*out*… a way to remember them. Easy!

phrasal verbs   *to use*   *like – for example*
                                                                 such as
   to make use of .
   to come up with – suggest   to opt for
                        find
                            an idea
   to work out .
        ⌐ find a solution.

7/8

✓ H/W tues

Part 3

For questions **17–24**, read the text below. Use the word given in capitals at the end of some of the lines to form a word that fits in the gap **in the same line**. There is an example at the beginning **(0)**.

Write your answers **IN CAPITAL LETTERS** on the separate answer sheet.

Example:

0	I	N	C	R	E	A	S	I	N	G	L	Y					

Too many climbers on Mount Everest

grammar fits

spelling

Mount Everest in Nepal is becoming **(0)** …….. popular as a destination **INCREASE**

favourable

for adventure tourism. During the month of May, **(17)** …….. weather **FAVOUR** ✓

presents a number of safe opportunities to make the climb. As a result, the

unexpected

sheer number of climbers has brought an **(18)** …….. problem, potentially **EXPECT**

even more dangerous than low temperatures and changeable weather –

overcrowded conditions. The fact that there are so many climbers, many

beginners

of them complete **(19)** …….. , means that at times people are queuing for **BEGIN**

hours to reach the summit.

This hazard has led to calls for stricter assessments of new learner climbers,

desperation

as in their **(20)** …….. to reach the mountain's summit such inexperienced **DESPERATE**

climbers are sometimes ignoring the advice of their Nepalese guides, which

endanger

may **(21)** …….. everyone's lives. *May + verb.* **DANGER** -

solution

Perhaps one **(22)** …….. would be to make the charges for climbing **SOLVE**

the mountain so high that only a few people could afford the climb. Or

alternatively

(23) …….. , one could ban the use of artificial oxygen and local guides, **ALTERNATE**

mountainance.

leaving Everest to the very best **(24)** …….. . Extreme, maybe, but it may just **MOUNTAIN**

noun. *mountaineers.*

prove necessary. R

verb, noun
adverb, adjective.
negative version.
prefix.
thing
person

7/8

11

Part 4

For questions **25–30**, complete the second sentence so that it has a similar meaning to the first sentence, using the word given. **Do not change the word given.** You must use between **three** and **six** words, including the word given. Here is an example (**0**).

Example:

0 James would only speak to the head of department alone.

ON

James .... to the head of department alone.

The gap can be filled with the words 'insisted on speaking', so you write:

Example:	**0**	INSISTED ON SPEAKING

Write **only** the missing words **IN CAPITAL LETTERS on the separate answer sheet.**

---

25 'You should stop your children watching so much television,' Mary's sister told her.

   LET

   Mary's sister advised her .not to let. *her children watch* ✓ .... so much television.

26 The local council wants to impose a ban on driving at more than 30 kilometres per hour anywhere in this area.

   ILLEGAL

   make it ✗

   Make sthg illegal

   The local council wants to become illegal to drive. .... at more than 30 kilometres per hour anywhere in this area.

   introduce a law

27 Tom missed his plane because he was late leaving for the airport.

   TIME

   Tom had left in time ✓

   If only .... for the airport, he wouldn't have missed his plane.

28 The guidelines for the appointment of new staff need to be thoroughly revised.

THOROUGH

There needs ~~to be a thorough~~ revision of ✓ .... the guidelines for the appointment of new staff.

29 The employment rate rose gradually as the economy began to recover.

(statistical increase

a rise in sthg

GRADUAL

There ~~was a gradual rise of~~ in ✗ .... the employment rate as the economy began to recover.

30 The change in the company's logo didn't make any difference to the majority of its customers.

CONSEQUENCE ✓

The change in the company's logo ~~was not any consequence~~ .... to the majority of its customers.

13

Part 5

You are going to read an article about a famous psychologist. For questions **31–36**, choose the answer (**A**, **B**, **C** or **D**) which you think fits best according to the text.

Mark your answers **on the separate answer sheet**.

Jean Piaget

Jean Piaget, the pioneering Swiss philosopher and psychologist, became famous for his theories on child development. A child prodigy, he became interested in the scientific study of nature at an early age. He developed a special fascination for biology, having some of his work published before graduating from high school. When, aged 10, his observations led to questions that could be answered only by access to the university library, Piaget wrote and published some notes on the sighting of an albino sparrow in the hope that this would persuade the librarian to stop treating him like a child. It worked. Piaget was launched on a path that led to his doctorate in zoology and a lifelong conviction that the way to understand anything is to know how it evolves.

Piaget went on to spend much of his professional life listening to and watching children, and poring over reports of researchers who were doing the same. He found, to put it succinctly, that children don't think like adults. After thousands of interactions with young people often barely old enough to talk, Piaget began to suspect that behind their cute and seemingly illogical utterances were thought processes that had their own kind of order and their own special logic. Albert Einstein, the renowned physicist, deemed this a discovery 'so simple that only a genius could have thought of it'.

Piaget's insight opened a new window into the inner workings of the mind. Several new fields of science, among them developmental psychology and cognitive theory, came into being as a result of his research. Although not an educational reformer, he championed a way of thinking about children that provided the foundation for today's education reform movements. One might say that Piaget was the first to take children's thinking seriously. Others who shared this respect for children may have fought harder for immediate change in schools, but Piaget's influence on education remains deeper and more pervasive.

Piaget has been revered by generations of teachers inspired by the belief that children are not empty vessels to be filled with knowledge, as traditional academic thinking had it, but active builders of knowledge – little scientists who are constantly creating and testing their own theories of the world. And while he may not be as famous as Sigmund Freud, Piaget's contribution to psychology may be longer lasting. As computers and the Internet give children greater autonomy to explore ever larger digital worlds, the ideas he pioneered become ever more relevant.

In the 1940s, working in Alfred Binet's child-psychology lab in Paris, Piaget noticed that children of the same age, regardless of their background or gender, made comparable errors on true–false intelligence tests. Back in Switzerland, the young scientist began watching children play, scrupulously recording their words and actions as their minds raced to find reasons for why things are the way they are. Piaget recognised that a five-year-old's beliefs, while not correct by any adult criterion, are not 'incorrect' either. They are entirely sensible and coherent within the framework of the child's 'way of knowing'. In Piaget's view, classifying them as 'true' or 'false' misses the point and shows a lack of respect for the child. What Piaget was after was a theory that could find coherence and ingenuity in the child's justification, and evidence of a kind of explanatory principle that stands young children in very good stead when they don't know enough or don't have enough skill to handle the kind of explanation that grown-ups prefer.

The core of Piaget's work is his belief that looking carefully at how children acquire knowledge sheds light on how adults think and understand the world. Whether this has, in fact, led to deeper understanding remains, like everything about Piaget, contentious. In recent years, Piaget has been vigorously challenged by the current emphasis on viewing knowledge as an intrinsic property of the brain. Ingenious experiments have demonstrated that newborn infants already have some of the knowledge that Piaget believed children constructed. But for those of us who still see Piaget as the giant in the field of cognitive theory, the disparity between what the baby brings and what the adult has is so immense that the new discoveries do not significantly reduce the gap, only increase the mystery.

31   In the first paragraph, the writer suggests that as a child Piaget

  A   was particularly eager to teach others about animals.
  B   was confident his research would help other children.
  C   was already certain about the career he would follow.
  D   was determined that nothing should hold back his progress.

32   In quoting Einstein, the writer is

  A   questioning the simplicity of Piaget's ideas.
  B   supporting the conclusion that Piaget reached.
  C   suggesting that Piaget's research methods were unprecedented.
  D   recommending a less complicated approach than Piaget's.

33   In the third paragraph, the writer puts forward the view that

  A   Piaget's work with children was difficult to put to a practical use.
  B   Piaget's theories about children were less revolutionary than he thought.
  C   Piaget laid the basis for our current understanding of how children's minds work.
  D   Piaget was actually committed to radical change in the education system.

34   The phrase 'empty vessels' (paragraph 4) refers to

  A   why children should be encouraged to study more independently.
  B   what traditional academic theory said about children and learning.
  C   how teachers can increase children's motivation to learn.
  D   the kind of knowledge that children need to acquire.

35   The writer says Piaget was unwilling to categorise children's ideas as true or false because

  A   he realised that the reasoning behind a child's statement was more important.
  B   he knew that this could have long-term effects on a child.
  C   he felt that this did not reflect what happens in real life.
  D   he felt that children are easily influenced by what adults have told them.

36   What does the writer conclude about newer theories that have appeared?

  A   They completely undermine Piaget's ideas.
  B   They put greater emphasis on scientific evidence.
  C   They are an interesting addition to the body of knowledge.
  D   They are based on flawed research.

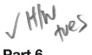

Part 6

You are going to read four contributions to an online debate about advertising. For questions
37–40, choose from the contributions **A–D**. The contributions may be chosen more than once.
Mark your answers **on the separate answer sheet**.

The role of advertising in society today

A   Almost all public spaces nowadays have advertisements in sight, and all forms of media, from
newspapers to the cinema to the Internet, are filled with adverts. This all-pervasive presence reflects
the value of advertising to us. Without it, businesses of all types and sizes would struggle to inform
potential customers about the products or services they provide, and consumers would be unable
to make informed assessments when looking for products to buy and services to use. Without
advertising, the promotion of products and practices that contribute to our physical and psychological
well-being – medicines to treat minor ailments, insurance schemes to protect us, clothes and
cosmetics to make us look and feel better – would be infinitely more problematic than it is. And
without advertisements and the aspirations represented in them, the world would be a far duller place.

B   Advertising is everywhere, and it's often so subtle that we don't realise it's there at some level of our
consciousness. The ultimate aim, of course, is to get us to buy things, regardless of whether it makes
sense for us to do so. In fact, adverts mostly impair rational decision-making. A recent study in the
UK found that 90% of customers failed to understand the truth about what was on offer in adverts for
broadband internet services. This irrational dimension is evident in the success advertisers enjoy not
only in getting us to buy products that, directly or indirectly, cause physical damage to us, but also
in raising our expectations about what our lives should be like – expectations that inevitably imply
something is wrong with us if we don't meet them. Having said this, advertising is fundamental to the
workings of modern economies, so the chances are that it will only continue to grow in significance.

C   There is a tendency to underestimate people's intelligence and to invest advertising with powers
it doesn't have. Certain dubious techniques have been banned – like the use of subliminal images
shown so quickly that viewers don't consciously realise they've seen them – but other forms of
advertising are simply manifestations of creativity. Audiences understand this and are able to enjoy
adverts without falling prey to some complex deception. They know that an advert tells them a product
exists and suggests they might benefit from having it. They don't expect it to provide objective details,
confirming why they should or should not go ahead with a purchase. They are also smart enough to
know that what they see in advertisements is fiction and, therefore, not something they should feel
bad about if they don't have it. The bottom line, however, is that advertising helps the wheels of the
economy to turn, a crucial role which societies are likely to depend on for the foreseeable future.

D   Advertising is a worldwide, multi-billion dollar industry and inevitably tends to favour large businesses,
which can afford advertising costs, rather than smaller companies, which can't. In that way, it makes
life ever more difficult for that sector of the economy – small and medium-sized businesses – which
is the key to a nation's prosperity. Advertising also encourages certain patterns of consumption – fast
food, cars, labour-saving devices and so on – which characterise a sedentary lifestyle and undermine
physical well-being, while also generating a sense of inadequacy and unhappiness among people
who feel inferior if they don't possess a product or conform to certain ideas of what is 'beautiful'
or 'cool'. And far from providing consumers with clear, reliable information enabling them to make
sensible decisions about what to spend their money on, advertisers use underhand methods to
confuse and manipulate feelings and thoughts.

Which contributor

expresses a different view from the others about the impact that advertising has on a country's economy? | **37** | D | ✓

has a different opinion from the others on the extent to which advertising helps people to make choices? | **38** | B | ✗

takes a similar view to contributor D about the influence advertising can have on people's self-esteem? | **39** | B | ✓

expresses a different opinion from contributor B regarding public awareness of how advertising works? | **40** | C | ✓

Part 7

You are going to read a magazine article about whale sharks. Six paragraphs have been removed from the article. Choose from the paragraphs **A–G** the one which fits each gap (**41–46**). There is one extra paragraph which you do not need to use.

Mark your answers **on the separate answer sheet.**

Secrets of the deep

Until recently, little was known about the movements of the whale shark. But a pioneering project is shedding new light on this ocean giant. Project scientist Jonathan Green reports.

When an animal the size of a very large double-decker bus – the largest fish in the ocean – makes a sudden 90° turn, it has to be for a good reason. As the satellite tracks started to come in from whale sharks which we had tagged off the Galapagos Islands, they clearly showed that as the sharks were swimming away from the islands, they were all reaching a certain point and then making a very abrupt change in direction.

41	C

That, among other things, was what The Galapagos Whale Shark Project was attempting to find out. Established to study the population of sharks that visits the islands each year, the primary aim of the research was to find out more about whale shark movements on a local scale.

42	E

This involved two main processes. To begin with, we had to be able to identify individual sharks. We used a modified version of photo software initially developed for the mapping of stars and deep-space objects. This worked because the characteristic white spots of the whale shark resemble the human fingerprint in that each pattern is individually unique. By running photographs of the sharks' sides through the software, we could characterise the patterns of spots, and figure out which shark was which.

43	G

We also attached tags to the sharks to track their movements. This was done by inserting a small dart through the thick skin into a fatty layer beneath using a pneumatic spear gun and then tethering the tags with a piece of steel cable. They were intended to be towed alongside or above the dorsal fin in order to break the surface and transmit data by satellite. But getting the tags to stay on was easier said than done. For reasons unknown, some came off in less than 24 hours.

44	A

The sharks used common departure routes soon after we had tagged them. They headed due north, following a series of sea fissures until they reached the Galapagos Rift Valley system. This zone is where the divergence of two oceanic plates has created a rift system similar to that which runs through eastern Africa. Many reached the margin between the two plates and most then turned west.

45	B X F

Conversely, one juvenile female's track was astounding, overlaying almost perfectly the rift system as it runs west. It's clear that she and the other whale sharks are using geological features as route indicators, just as motorists use, say, familiar buildings. But how the sharks perceive such features thousands of meters below on the ocean floor is as yet unresolved.

46	D

The theory we are working on is that the Earth's magnetic field reverses its polarity intermittently over the course of time, thus supplying a source of directional information. Fault systems, rift valleys, ocean trenches and plate margins all emit a distinct magnetic signature that can be used by whale sharks and other species as a virtual map.

A There may be a number of explanations: the sharks might have rubbed up against rocks, or the tags may have been ripped off by associated species, such as silky sharks, that mistook them for prey. Having begun with a 1.8-metre tether, we shortened this to 1.3 metres, which seemed to be more effective.

B After three months, all the sharks that had retained their tags proceeded to head south. They converged on three mountain chains that run westwards from the edge of Peru's continental shelf. There, one by one, they shed their tags and continued on to destinations unknown.

C However, it wasn't until we overlaid them onto a map of the sea floor that we saw that these movements were apparently in response to geological features deep in the ocean that the sharks couldn't possibly see. It became clear that they must somehow be using faults, fissures and plate boundaries. But how?

D After all, the marine environment, in comparison to that on land, has few apparent points of reference. The waters are often murky and the maximum penetration of light only extends into the upper levels. So how do marine creatures navigate over long distances?

E We undertook one of the most ambitious whale shark programmes to date. The fieldwork was carried out in three 15-day sorties.

F The frequency of transmissions from the tags depended on the behaviour of the individual sharks. Some spent a lot of time on or near the surface, and their tags reported on a regular basis. Others, such as the single male we tagged, spent a great deal of the time diving – for six weeks we didn't receive a single transmission.

G If spotted at the same location at a later date, or a different location, the shark was 'recaptured' on a database, which stores photos of whale sharks from around the globe, thus providing details of their movements geographically and over time.

Part 8

You are going to read an article about employees who do some or all of their work from home. For questions **47–56**, choose from the sections (**A–D**). The sections may be chosen more than once.

Mark your answers **on the separate answer sheet**.

In which section are the following mentioned?

the mistaken view that physical proximity at work automatically ensures good supervision	**47**	C ✓
the fact that the proportion of home workers in the labour force has not matched expectations	**48**	A ✓
the risk of an employer making unreasonable demands on a home worker	**49**	D ✓
the fact that staff retention increases in firms that encourage home working	**50**	B ✓
the duty of firms not to dismiss requests to work at home out of hand	**51**	D ✗ A
one of the main obstacles to home working in employers' minds being the fear of loss of direct control	**52**	C ✓
personal circumstances increasing the likelihood of an individual being allowed to work at home	**53**	A ✓
the wider benefits that home working brings to the community	**54**	A ✗ C
the advisability of ensuring that home workers are not putting in excessive hours	**55**	D ✓
a reduction in expenditure on premises as a result of home working	**56**	B ✓

The Rise of Home Working

A Whether you call it working from home, telecommuting or home-working, it's a growing market. Banks, call centres, councils, software companies, law firms, PR agencies: all are increasingly allowing their staff to do it at least part-time. British Telecom, the pioneer of home working in Britain, now has 65,000 flexible workers, of whom 10,000 do not come into the office at all. However, we're still a long way from the dreams of 25 years ago, which imagined offices emptying of everyone who didn't operate a machine or wield a mop. So how do you get on the home-working bandwagon? In some countries, if you have a child under 16, or 18 if they are disabled, in a sense you have a head start. Employers in Britain are legally obliged at least to consider your case if you ask to work flexibly, and that could include working at home for at least part of the week. They must also consider an application if you are caring for a friend or a family member. But even if none of those apply, you are still likely to have a strong case – if you can persuade your company to listen.

B Not only do home workers cut down on the need for large offices, they are often vastly more productive. American studies show a 30–40% increase. Noel Hodson, a key proponent of home working, suggests that this is at least partly down to the removal of the daily commute: 'What we found was that most of the time saved went back into work. These workers valued their new lifestyle and to protect it they did more work.' Companies that offer flexible working also find it easier to attract staff, and to hang on to them. At British Telecom, at least 97% of women who take maternity leave come back to work afterwards, against a national average of about half that. The downtime, the recruitment, the instruction of each person at a very moderate estimate would be around £10,000. So, not only are they creating a more socially integrated company in line with government guidelines, they're saving £5m–£6m on skill losses.

C And there are bonuses for society too. Home working encourages a more diverse labour force, introducing to the world of work, sometimes for the first time, not just carers but disabled people or those who live in remote locations. Then there's the reduction in pollution and greenhouse gases. So if home working is so great, why aren't we all doing it? 'The issues are human, not technological,' says Peter Thomson of the Telework Association. 'For the past 200 years we have been in an environment where people get together in the same place to work and a manager stands there and watches what they do.' So the last barriers are attitudinal, but it's a myth that someone is in total charge of what people do just because they are all working in the same location. Most managers who are worried about this kind of thing are actually holed up in their offices and rarely interact with their people. Merely turning up is a really poor performance indicator.

D Mark Thomas runs a PR consultancy whose employees work at home. 'We've come up with measures of performance that are more to do with what they produce than with desk time. This is the way forward,' he says. Some managers are concerned that their home workers might go shopping during the 'working day'. This goes against the idea of flexible working since hours shouldn't matter so long as the required productivity is there. The concern still remains whether some employees will abuse this, but the same technology that makes it possible to escape the office makes it harder to get away from your boss, which is surely true even if you work in an office. It's well known that some managers insist on interrupting their underlings' evenings and weekends with 'urgent' enquiries that could easily wait. So, many of us are already on call 24/7. However, the great thing about technology is that it has an 'off button'. The best employers will not just expect you to use it, but worry if you don't.

WRITING (1 hour 30 minutes)

Part 1

You **must** answer this question. Write your answer in **220–260** words in an appropriate style.

1   Your class has listened to a radio discussion on how more young people can be encouraged to study science. You have made the notes below:

> **Ways of encouraging young people to study science:**
> - advertising
> - school programmes
> - government grants

> Some opinions expressed in the discussion:
>
> "You never see positive images of young scientists on TV, just pop stars or actors."
>
> "Science lessons should be more practical and fun."
>
> "If young people see science as a career, they'll want to study it."

Write an essay discussing **two** of the points in your notes. You should **explain which way would be more effective in encouraging young people to study science, providing reasons** to support your opinion.

You may, if you wish, make use of the opinions expressed in the discussion, but you should use your own words as far as possible.

Part 2

Write an answer to **one** of the questions **2–4** in this part. Write your answer in **220–260** words in an appropriate style.

---

2   You recently helped to organise an arts day in your area, promoting local musicians and artists through performances, workshops and exhibitions. You read the article below in a local paper:

> ### Local arts day – a disappointment
>
> Last week's arts day didn't attract many people, had limited appeal to young people and was a waste of council money.

You disagree with the negative opinions expressed by the reporter, and decide to write a letter to the Editor, explaining why you disagree and saying what you feel was achieved on the day.

Write your **letter**. You do not need to include postal addresses.

3   You are on the Student Committee at the college where you study. A year ago, the college gave the Committee some money to start a student website. The aims of the website were to inform students about local events, to publicise college clubs, and to review products of interest to students.

The Principal has asked you for a report explaining whether the website has met its aims and saying why the website should continue to have financial support.

Write your **report**.

4   You are a university student and you want to spend a month doing work experience at an international company. You decide to write a letter to the Recruitment Manager at the company explaining why you want to do work experience there and saying how the company would also benefit.

Write your **letter**.

LISTENING (approximately 40 minutes)

Part 1

You will hear three different extracts. For questions **1–6**, choose the answer (**A**, **B** or **C**) which fits best according to what you hear. There are two questions for each extract.

Extract One

You hear two friends talking about a new office building.

1 The woman says that in the building some people are having difficulty

   A coping with the new technology.

   B adjusting to a new concept of work.

   C working without clear supervision.

2 She thinks one effect of people moving around the building will be to

   A promote physical as well as mental well-being.

   B create a more productive work force.

   C provide useful contact with other employees.

Extract Two

You hear two friends discussing business travel.

3 The woman believes that in future companies should

   A fly only with airlines that have an eco-friendly policy.

   B concentrate on the use of video conferencing.

   C reduce overall levels of executive travel.

4 The man thinks that the prime consideration for transport providers should be

   A increasing revenue.

   B thinking long-term.

   C creating jobs.

Extract Three

You hear two friends talking about some research.

5   What is the man's attitude to the research?

    A   He is doubtful about the methods used.

    B   He is surprised by its findings.

    C   He is dismissive of the concept behind it.

6   During the discussion, the woman reveals her

    A   sympathy towards the subjects of the experiments.

    B   interest in complex human behaviour.

    C   admiration for the originality of the research.

Part 2

You will hear a man called Steven Kane giving a presentation about research into a cargo of children's bath-toys which were lost at sea. For questions **7–14**, complete the sentences with a word or short phrase.

BATH-TOY CARGO

Of the four kinds of bath-toy lost at sea, Steven thinks the [**7**   ]

had the most surprising colour.

The subject Steven was teaching when he first read about the bath-toys was

[**8**   ]

In Alaska, Steven heard of a lost consignment of [**9**   ] ,

some of which turned up alongside the bath-toys.

Steven discovered that the bath-toys are used by scientists known as

[**10**   ] in their research.

Steven says that the findings obtained by researchers were immediately useful to

the [**11**   ] industry.

Steven mentions the particular case of a [**12**   ] adversely

affected by plastic pollutants in the sea.

Steven regarded the factory that he traced in China as the bath-toys'

[**13**   ] .

Steven travelled on something called an [**14**   ] on his

journey across the Arctic.

Part 3

You will hear part of an interview in which two scientists called Jessica Conway and Paul Flower are talking about exploration and discovery. For questions **15–20**, choose the answer (**A**, **B**, **C** or **D**) which fits best according to what you hear.

15   In response to the idea that everything has already been discovered Jessica emphasises
    A   the potential for further marine exploration.
    B   the precision of modern satellite technology.
    C   the inaccuracy of modern mapping techniques.
    D   the number of recent discoveries.

16   Regarding new species found around underwater craters, Jessica says that
    A   they are being discovered less often these days.
    B   they are more abundant in certain locations.
    C   it is difficult to estimate possible numbers.
    D   there are problems classifying them.

17   When asked about geographical discoveries in general, Paul and Jessica agree that scientists need to
    A   make regular reassessments of their work.
    B   compare their respective results.
    C   recognise their limitations.
    D   promote their findings.

18   What does Paul say about walking where no one has ever walked before?
    A   It recharges his tired mind.
    B   It makes him feel he is unique.
    C   It gives him a sense of belonging.
    D   It helps him forget physical discomfort.

19   When asked about others visiting remote areas, Paul
    A   supports the public's right to experience them.
    B   expresses his concern at growing urbanisation.
    C   suggests it would benefit local communities.
    D   criticises the attitude of some tourists.

20   In Paul's view, future generations will
    A   only need to go online to experience the thrill of adventure.
    B   have to reduce travel for environmental reasons.
    C   be less interested in the concept of exploration.
    D   still be attracted to isolated places.

Part 4

You will hear five short extracts in which people are talking about taking up a new sport.

TASK ONE

For questions **21–25**, choose from the list (**A–H**) why each speaker took up their particular sport.

TASK TWO

For questions **26–30**, choose from the list (**A–H**) what advice each speaker gives about taking up a sport.

While you listen you must complete both tasks.

A	to make new friends
B	as the result of recommendations
C	to get fit
D	for the travel opportunities
E	as a personal challenge
F	for the thrill of competing
G	to improve a skill
H	as a result of discovering a talent

Speaker 1	21
Speaker 2	22
Speaker 3	23
Speaker 4	24
Speaker 5	25

A	Stick to your training routine.
B	Don't let it rule your life.
C	Believe in yourself.
D	Get reliable assistance.
E	Follow a strict diet.
F	Try to be a good role model.
G	Don't expect instant rewards.
H	Continue to push to new limits.

Speaker 1	26
Speaker 2	27
Speaker 3	28
Speaker 4	29
Speaker 5	30

SPEAKING (15 minutes)

There are two examiners. One (the interlocutor) conducts the test, providing you with the necessary materials and explaining what you have to do. The other examiner (the assessor) is introduced to you, but then takes no further part in the interaction.

Part 1 (2 minutes)

The interlocutor first asks you and your partner a few questions. The interlocutor asks candidates for some information about themselves, then widens the scope of the questions by asking about e.g. candidates' leisure activities, studies, travel and daily life. Candidates are expected to respond to the interlocutor's questions and listen to what their partner has to say.

Part 2 (a one-minute 'long turn' for each candidate, plus a 30-second response from the second candidate)

You are each given the opportunity to talk for about a minute, and to comment briefly after your partner has spoken.

   The interlocutor gives you a set of pictures and asks you to talk about them for about one minute. It is important to listen carefully to the interlocutor's instructions. The interlocutor then asks your partner a question about your pictures and your partner responds briefly.

   You are then given another set of pictures to look at. Your partner talks about these pictures for about one minute. This time the interlocutor asks you a question about your partner's pictures and you respond briefly.

Part 3 (4 minutes)

In this part of the test, you and your partner are asked to talk together. The interlocutor places some text prompts on the table between you. This stimulus provides the basis for a discussion. The interlocutor explains what you have to do.

Part 4 (5 minutes)

The interlocutor asks some further questions, which leads to a more general discussion of what you have talked about in Part 3. You may comment on your partner's answers if you wish.

Test 2

READING AND USE OF ENGLISH (1 hour 30 minutes)

Part 1

For questions **1–8**, read the text below and decide which answer (**A, B, C** or **D**) best fits each gap. There is an example at the beginning (**0**).
Mark your answers **on the separate answer sheet**.

Example:

0 A balance   **B** record   **C** income   **D** profit

| 0 | A ▆ | B ☐ | C ☐ | D ☐ |

Promotion is good for your health

A recent study suggests that being promoted isn't just good for your bank **(0)** ..A....., it's also good for your health. Researchers found that those who work in jobs with better promotion **(1)** ..D.... are less likely to develop serious illnesses. Specifically, those working in departments with double the average promotion **(2)** ..B.... had a twenty percent better chance of escaping serious illness.

The researchers **(3)** ..B.... into account factors such as family background, pre-existing medical conditions and educational level. **(4)** ..C....., they could be confident that the lower occurrences of illness were not simply due to a healthier or more **(5)** ..A.... upbringing.

The results seem to **(6)** ..D.... earlier studies showing that people who win prestigious awards, such as an Oscar or Nobel Prize during their career, have a tendency to outlive those who are less fortunate. As the author of the report says, 'When our findings are put together with the large body of other **(7)** ..B.... literature, there is little **(8)** ..A.... that achieving a higher position at work is good for the health.'

5/
8

1 **A** forecasts   **B** advances   **C** predictions   **D** prospects

2 **A** scale   **B** rate   **C** degree   **D** ratio

3 **A** set   **B** took   **C** put   **D** made

4 **A** Anyway   **B** Moreover   **C** Consequently   **D** Admittedly

5 **A** privileged   **B** preferred   **C** entitled   **D** honoured

6 **A** call for   **B** go over   **C** back up   **D** lead to

7 **A** related   **B** combined   **C** referred   **D** incorporated

8 **A** hesitation   **B** question   **C** reservation   **D** opposition

Handwritten notes:

2 possibilities
Meaning → ⌈ guesswork   LI
           ⌊ collocation.

grammar fit.

what type of word.
adjective.

related literature

to be | little question that | something is true.
        no
        └ there is.....

Part 2

For questions **9–16**, read the text below and think of the word which best fits each gap. Use only **one** word in each gap. There is an example at the beginning (**0**).

Write your answers **IN CAPITAL LETTERS on the separate answer sheet**.

Example: | **0** | N | O | | | | | | | | | | | | | | | | |

Handwriting

About six months ago, I realised I had **(0)** ..NO... idea what the handwriting of a good friend of mine looked like. We had always communicated by email and text but never by a handwritten letter. And it struck me that we are at a moment **(9)** .... *when* handwriting seems to be about to vanish from our lives altogether. **(10)** .... *At* some point in recent years, it stopped **(11)** .... *as* a necessary and inevitable intermediary between people – a means by **(12)** .... *which* individuals communicate with each other, putting a little bit of their personality **(13)** .... *to* the form of the message as they press the ink-bearing point onto the paper. It has started to become just **(14)** .... *one* among many options, often considered unattractive and elaborate.

For each of us, the act of putting marks on paper with ink goes back as **(15)** .... *far* as we can remember. Our handwriting, like ourselves, seems always to have been there. But now, given that most of us communicate via email and text, have we lost **(16)** .... *something* crucial to the human experience?

Part 3

For questions **17–24**, read the text below. Use the word given in capitals at the end of some of the lines to form a word that fits in the gap **in the same line**. There is an example at the beginning (**0**). Write your answers **IN CAPITAL LETTERS on the separate answer sheet**.

Example: | 0 | T | R | A | N | S | F | O | R | M | A | T | I | O | N | | | | |

Modernising a museum

The Ashmolean Museum in Oxford, England – the world's oldest university

museum – has recently gone through a major **(0)** .... The architects   **TRANSFORM**

wanted to create a new space that would make the museum one of the

world's most important and **(17)** .... cultural showcases.   **INNOVATE**

innovative

The collections in the museum are absolutely **(18)** .... and cover the   **STAND**

✗ standard

cultures of east and west, charting the aspirations of mankind from the

prehistoric era to the present day. The approach that was adopted was

based on the idea that **(19)** .... that have shaped our modern societies   **CIVILISE**

civilisations

did not develop in isolation but were part of a complex interrelated world.

Every object has a **(20)** .... story to tell, and these are gradually uncovered   **SIGNIFY**

significant

through tracing the journey of ideas and influences across time and

continents.

People who knew the old museum say it has **(21)** .... an amazing   **GO**

undergone

makeover. The new layout **(22)** .... people to appreciate the objects   **ABLE**

enables

fully; it is **(23)** .... to everyone, from school children to academic   **ACCESS**

accessible

scholars, so **(24)** .... to all those involved in redesigning this wonderful   **CONGRATULATE**

congratulations.

treasure house.

Part 4

For questions **25–30**, complete the second sentence so that it has a similar meaning to the first sentence, using the word given. **Do not change the word given.** You must use between **three** and **six** words, including the word given. Here is an example (**0**).

Example:

0 James would only speak to the head of department alone.

ON

James .... to the head of department alone.

The gap can be filled with the words 'insisted on speaking', so you write:

Example:	0		INSISTED ON SPEAKING

Write **only** the missing words **IN CAPITAL LETTERS on the separate answer sheet.**

---

25 The other students don't mind whether you give your presentation on Thursday or Friday.

DIFFERENCE

It .makes no difference. ~~to~~ the other students whether you give your presentation on Thursday or Friday.

26 'What are you thinking of doing for the college's centenary celebration?' the tutor asked the students.

MIND

The tutor asked the students what *they had got in mind* .... for the college's centenary celebration.

27 Dr. Ramesh's colleagues regarded him so highly that they forgave his inability to remember people's names.

HELD

Dr. Ramesh *was held* .... by his colleagues that they forgave his inability to remember people's names.

28 As learning new languages had never been a problem for her, Katy didn't expect to have any difficulties when she went to live abroad.

COME

Learning new languages had ....always come easily to............... her so Katy didn't expect to have any difficulties when she went to live abroad.

29 I think we owe this passenger an apology, as she was apparently given incorrect train times by our call centre staff.

MISINFORMED

I think we owe this passenger an apology, as she seems ......misinformed about.................. train times by our call centre staff.

30 If her party wins the election, which is unlikely, she'll become President.

EVENT

In the ....X.......................... the election, she'll become President.

Part 5

You are going to read an extract from a novel. For questions **31–36**, choose the answer
(**A**, **B**, **C** or **D**) which you think fits best according to the text.
Mark your answers **on the separate answer sheet**.

Howard's Career as a Palaeontologist

Howard became a palaeontologist because of a rise in interest rates when he was six years old. His
father, a cautious man with a large mortgage and thoughts focussed merely on how the economic
situation would affect him, announced that the projected holiday to Spain was no longer feasible. A
chalet was rented on the English coast instead and thus, on a dank August afternoon, Howard picked
up a coiled fossil shell, called an ammonite, on the beach.

He knew for a long time that he wanted to become a palaeontologist, and towards the end of his
time at university he became clear as to what sort of palaeontologist he wanted to be. He found the
focus of his interest reaching further and further back in time. The more spectacular areas were not
for him, he realised, turning his back on the Jurassic, on dinosaurs. He was drawn particularly to the
beginnings, to that ultimate antiquity where everything is decided, from which, against all odds, we
derive. So he studied delicate creatures revealed on the surface of grey rocks.

Work on his doctoral thesis came to an end, and, he knew, possibly a bitter one. Would he get a job?
Would he get a job in the sort of institution he sought? He was far from being without self-esteem and
knew that his potential was good. But he knew that those who deserve do not always get, and that
while the objectives of science may be pure and uncompromising, the process of appointment to an
academic position is not. When the Assistant Lectureship at Tavistock College in London came up,
he applied at once, though without high hopes.

On the morning of Howard's interview, the professor who would chair the panel had a row with his
wife. As a consequence he left home in a state of irritation and inattention, drove his car violently into
a gatepost and ended up in the Casualty Department of the local hospital. The interview took place
without him and without the support he had intended to give to a candidate who had been a student
of his.

The professor who replaced him on the panel was a hated colleague, whose main concern was to
oppose the appointment of his enemy's protégé; he was able to engineer without much difficulty that
Howard got the job. Howard, surprised at the evident favouritism from a man he did not know, was
fervently grateful until, months later, a colleague kindly enlightened him as to the correct interpretation
of events. Howard was only slightly chagrined. It would have been nice to think that he was the
obvious candidate, or that he had captivated those present with his ability and personality. But by
then the only thing that really mattered was that he had the job and that he could support himself by
doing the sort of work he wanted to do.

He often found himself contrasting the orderly nature of his professional life – where the pursuit of
scientific truth was concerned, it was possible to plan a course of action and carry it out – with the
anarchy of private concerns. The world teems with people who can determine the quality of your
existence, and on occasion some total stranger can reach in and manipulate the entire narrative, as
Howard was to find when his briefcase, containing the notes for a lecture he was about to give, was
stolen at an Underground station.

Fuming, Howard returned to the college. He made an explanatory phone call and postponed the
lecture. He reported the theft to the appropriate authorities and then went for a restorative coffee. He
joined a colleague who was entertaining a visiting curator from the Natural History Museum in Nairobi.
And thus it was that Howard learnt of the recently acquired collection of fossils, as yet uncatalogued
and unidentified, the study of which would provide him with his greatest challenge and ensure his
professional future. But for the theft, but for that now benevolent stranger ... Within half an hour he
had dismantled and reassembled his plans. He would not go to a conference in Stockholm. He would
not spend a fortnight taking students on a field trip to Scotland. He would pull out every stop and
somehow scramble together the funds for a visit to the museum in Nairobi.

31 What is suggested about Howard's father in the first paragraph?

    A   He'd foreseen a change in the economic climate.
    B   He acted in character when cancelling the holiday.
    C   He'd never been in favour of holidays abroad.
    D   He tended to make decisions spontaneously.

32 What area of palaeontology did Howard develop a special interest in at university?

    A   the earliest life forms
    B   the dating of pieces of evidence
    C   the scale of pre-historic creatures
    D   the fragile beauty of many fossils

33 What concerned Howard about the chances of getting a job?

    A   his lack of work experience
    B   his uncertainty of his own worth
    C   that jobs were not always awarded on merit
    D   that jobs in his field were always in short supply

34 The result of Howard's job interview depended on

    A   a change of heart by a member of the panel.
    B   the relative strengths of the candidates.
    C   the performance of a favoured candidate.
    D   the conflict between two members of staff.

35 How did Howard feel when he learnt the truth about his appointment?

    A   pleased he would be so well paid
    B   unconcerned about why he got the job
    C   dismayed at not being the best candidate
    D   gratified to think he'd made a good impression

36 Over the text as a whole, the writer suggests that the course of Howard's career was determined to a large extent by

    A   a series of random coincidences.
    B   an interest developed in childhood.
    C   a belief in scientific certainties.
    D   a mix of hard work and academic success.

Part 6

You are going to read four extracts from online articles about sports psychology. For questions **37–40**, choose from the extracts **A–D**. The extracts may be chosen more than once.
Mark your answers **on the separate answer sheet.**

Sports psychology: a valid discipline?

A   **Dorothy Common**

Is the ever growing discipline of sports psychology contributing effectively to sporting performance or is it, as many people think, simply the art of 'stating the blindingly obvious'? I have certainly seen evidence that those in journalistic circles are yet to be fully convinced. And it is certainly true that sport psychologists should strive to increase the sophistication of their approaches to research, making use of more reliable scientific methods. Yet it's a shame that people should be so sceptical. Essentially, sports psychology asks this simple question: considering the undeniable role mental life plays in deciding the outcomes of our sporting efforts, why is mental training not incorporated to the equivalent degree into the athlete's typical training? If, say, a track sprinter is susceptible to letting their head get the better of them (temper issues, nerves, anxiety), then why should they spend their training just working on their strengths (the physical side)?

B   **Jahangir Khan**

There is a popular view, largely based on a well-known case with a prominent runner, that sports psychology is something for treating athletes with mental disorders. This has no basis in fact and stems from making assumptions based on a limited understanding of psychology and how it is used in applied settings. In my area of particular expertise, football, rugby and hockey, there exists a culture of what one psychologist calls 'folk psychology'. That is, there are usually individuals (typically an older dominant coach) who communicate non-scientific words of wisdom which, consciously or unconsciously, affect everyone, usually to detrimental effect in the long run. Think of a young player who is told to 'dig deep' and give it '110%' consistently. This gives a mental aspect to training that is non-scientific and misguided. But this is in stark contrast to the reality of modern day psychology research, which is based upon rigorous scientific methodologies.

C   **Brian D. Rossweller**

Research into sports psychology is increasingly evidence-based, using the gold standard methodology of 'randomized control group designs'. Nevertheless, using the term 'psychology' in relation to psychological efforts with athletes, especially those involved in team sports, can be both an asset and a hindrance to understanding the field. Psychology as a field has become much more acceptable in social life. It seems that every time a person flicks through the television channels they are likely to see a psychologist talking about something or other. Thus people tend to view psychologists, including those seen on sports programmes, as knowledgeable and as providing information useful to everyday life. However, the flip side is that most people know someone who sees a clinical psychologist or therapist for a mind-related problem. In our society there has been a stigma attached to such problems and so many people have attached negative connotations to seeing a psychologist and may misunderstand the nature of seeing a sports psychologist.

D   **Xiu Li**

There is still some distance between research and coaching practice. Sports psychology has been able to develop a relatively significant research base in the last fifteen years; aided by general experimental researchers often using athletes as an easily identifiable and obtainable population. Yet, as a practising sports psychologist I recently observed an athletics coach, whose reaction to a promising middle-distance runner losing a winning position on the last lap was to prioritise developing a sprint finish. What he didn't address was the fact that the runner failed to focus whenever he got overtaken. Then again, I also witnessed some baseball coaches doing some work - which I would have been proud of in my professional capacity - on assessing and profiling strengths and weaknesses, and also on performance anxiety. So things vary, and some trainers are clearly more knowledgeable than others. But it is not surprising that, as a result, public conceptions are confused on the issue.

Which expert

shares Khan's opinion on why public misconceptions about sports psychology have occurred?

| 37 | C |

has a different view from Khan on whether some psychological training used in team sports is helpful to the players?

| 38 | D |

has a different view from Rossweller on how the media regard sports psychologists?

| 39 | A |

has a different opinion from the other three experts on the current state of research in sports psychology?

| 40 | B | X |

Part 7

You are going to read a newspaper article about a new trend in the travel and tourism industry. Six paragraphs have been removed from the article. Choose from the paragraphs **A–G** the one which fits each gap (**41–46**). There is one extra paragraph which you do not need to use.
Mark your answers **on the separate answer sheet.**

Stargazing in East Africa

Jonathan Ford went to Tanzania on an 'astro-safari', which combines animal-watching with looking at the stars.

We are gathered about a campfire on the dusty edge of the Serengeti National Park. After a long day scanning the savannah for creatures with jaws, claws, tusks, the flames are comforting. Normally on one of these trips, this is the moment at which the day starts to wind down; when tourists compare the animals they've had the chance of seeing and capturing on film.

| 41 | E |

Amateur astronomy is enjoying a surge of popularity and remote hotels around the world are installing telescopes and hiring expert star guides. Nevertheless, when I first heard about the idea of an 'astro-safari', I was sceptical. Wasn't the whole point of going to Africa to look around at hyenas and gazelles, say, rather than up at constellations that have scarcely changed since our ancestors first struggled to stand upright?

| 42 | A |

So it was with certain qualms that I found myself in Tanzania, on one of the first such safaris in Africa. The plan was simple. We would spend four days travelling through the spectacular Ngorongoro crater and the highlands, before dropping down on to the plain, animal watching by day and stargazing by night. We would hit the Serengeti plains just as 1.5 million wildebeest were making their way across, accompanied by zebras and gazelles, one of east Africa's most thrilling sights.

| 43 | C |

We were in luck: Nick Howes, a science writer for the European Space Agency learnt to love astronomy at an

early age. A natural communicator, Howes promptly reassured us that degrees in astrophysics are all very well, but cutting-edge astronomy relies on the work of thousands of amateurs. They are just like us, but with better lenses and more patience.

| 44 | D |

The vocabulary, however, was alluringly alien: not just nebulae and supernovae, but globular clusters and Magellanic Clouds. Howes continued the astral tour even in daylight hours. To do so, he had brought with him a solar scope that you screw into a telescope. This allows you to look directly into the sun, and, if you are lucky, see the huge 'coronal mass injections' that spurt from the surface of our very own star.

| 45 | G |

In fact, 'seeing' here in the Serengeti – astronomer-speak for clarity – is among the best in the world. But it was the unexpected spectacles that caused the greatest delight: one evening, a great fireball streaked across the sky, seeming to plunge to earth some way to the south.

| 46 | B |

Appropriate perhaps, considering that this is the part of the world where mankind first lived and looked at the night sky. Within 24 hours of arriving, the raw tourist finds himself asking all the big questions – the origins of the universe, why life started here of all places … and the relative scariness of hyenas and asteroids. It was completely different to sitting in front of a TV screen where everything seemed more certain.

A Stars, unlike elephants and giraffes, can surely be seen any winter evening from anyone's back garden. And it was doubtful that anything could be learnt from peering through a telescope that some professor couldn't get across on a TV programme.

B We mobbed our guide with fretful questions. He shrugged and laughed. It could be a meteor. 'You have to get used to not knowing. That's the hardest part of the job,' he said. It was then I became aware of the point of being here.

C What was less clear was how our night-time viewing would go. Our group featured no one who could confidently say what they were looking at in the sky, so much depended on the astronomer accompanying us.

D Indeed, we learnt that Nik Szymanek, one of the world's finest astro-photographers, is a London Tube driver by day. Tom Boles, who has discovered more supernovas than anyone living, turns out to be a retired telecoms engineer.

E But here the banter is not of giraffe and rhino but of astronomical terms like quarks and parsecs. A particular constellation of stars known as Leo will be turning up, cloud permitting, later that night. Who will be awake? 'We won't be able to see it till about 3.30 in the morning,' says our guide, cheerily unfazed by the idea of staying up till dawn.

F My nonchalance didn't stand a chance against this passion and knowledge. I soon realised that the sky over my London home is a moth-eaten faded curtain compared with the lavishly studded dome that dominates the wilds of Africa. This is due, of course, to the total absence of light pollution.

G I wasn't sure whether it had been the right decision, even though seeing the animals at close range was thrilling. But then I saw the Carina Nebula, nothing but the faintest of glows to the naked eye but a furnace of throbbing scientific possibility when seen through the telescope.

Part 8

You are going to read an article about scientific interpretations of modern art. For questions **47–56**, choose from the sections (**A–D**). The sections may be chosen more than once.

Mark your answers **on the separate answer sheet**.

In which section does the writer...

mention certain viewers being able to relate to what artists had in mind?	47
refer to a doubt about the merit of a piece of artwork?	48
highlight a need for artists to strike the right balance?	49
indicate a possible reason for difficulty in reaching a consensus?	50
state that people may have a shallow reason for liking a piece of art?	51
suggest that some artists are aware of how they can satisfy the brain?	52
refer to a shift in her own perception?	53
point out shortcomings in a specific piece of research?	54
mention the possibility of extending the scope of an existing research area?	55
describe a procedure employed in the gathering of some scientific data?	56

A scientific view of modern art

Kat Austen investigates scientific research on modern art and why we appreciate it

A Standing in front of Jackson Pollock's *Summertime: Number 9A* one day I was struck by a strange feeling. What I once considered an ugly collection of random paint splatters now spoke to me as a joyous celebration of movement and energy. It was the first time a piece of abstract art had stirred my emotions. Like many, I used to dismiss these works as a waste of time and energy. How could anyone find meaning in what looked like a collection of colourful splodges thrown haphazardly at a canvas? Yet here I was, in London's Tate Modern gallery, moved by Pollock's work. So, why are we attracted to paintings and sculptures that seem to bear no relation to the physical world? Little did I know that researchers have already started to investigate this question. By studying the brain's responses to different paintings, they have been examining the way the mind perceives art, and how masterpieces hijack the brain's visual system.

B Studies in the emerging field of neuroaesthetics have already offered insights into many masterpieces. The blurred imagery of paintings of the Impressionist era towards the end of the 19th century seems to stimulate a part of the brain which is geared towards detecting threats in our rather blurry peripheral vision. The same part of the brain also plays a crucial role in our feelings and emotions, which might explain why many people find these pieces so moving. Could the same approach tell us anything about modern art, the defining characteristic of which has been to remove almost everything that could be literally interpreted? Although such works often sell for vast sums of money, they have attracted many sceptics, who claim that modern artists lack the skills or competence of the masters before them. Instead they believe that many people claim to like these works simply because they are in fashion.

C In an attempt to make sense of how we perceive art, scientists have designed experiments that play with volunteers' expectations of the pieces they are viewing. The volunteers viewed pairs of paintings – either creations by famous abstract artists or the doodles of infants, chimps and elephants. Then they had to judge which they liked best. A third of the paintings were given no captions, while the rest were labelled. The twist was that sometimes the labels were mixed up so that the volunteers might think they were viewing a chimp's messy brushstrokes, while they were actually seeing an abstract piece by a famous artist. Some sceptics might argue that it is impossible to tell the difference, but in each set of trials, the volunteers generally went for the work of the well-accepted human artists. Somehow it seems that the viewer can sense the artist's vision in these paintings, even if they can't explain why. Yet, the experiment did not explain how we detect the hand of the human artist, nor the reason why the paintings appeal to us. But how does the artist hold our attention with an image that bears no likeness to anything in the real world? Of course, each artist's unique style will speak to us in a different way, so there can be no single answer.

D A few studies have tackled the issue of how people process images, a case in point being Robert Pepperell's attempt to understand the way we deal with works which do not offer even the merest glimpse of a recognisable object for the brain to latch on to. But they may instead catch our attention through particularly well-proportioned compositions that appeal to the brain's visual system. We may also be drawn in by pieces that hit a specific point in the brain's ability to process complex scenes, which, in turn, may be why certain artists use a particular level of detail to please the brain. According to one psychologist, if there is too little detail we find the work boring, but too much complexity results in a kind of perceptual overload.

WRITING (1 hour 30 minutes)

Part 1

You **must** answer this question. Write your answer in **220–260** words in an appropriate style.

1   Your class has watched a studio discussion about factors which have contributed to the recent increase in international travel. You have made the notes below:

Factors contributing to the increase in international travel:
- methods of transport
- global business
- media

Some opinions expressed in the discussion:

"It's quicker to fly abroad than to take a train to the north of my country!"

"My company has offices in 12 different countries."

"People have developed a love of other cultures through TV and film."

Write an essay for your tutor discussing **two** of the factors in your notes. You should **explain which factor has contributed more to the increase in international travel**, **providing reasons** to support your opinion.

You may, if you wish, make use of the opinions expressed in the discussion, but you should use your own words as far as possible.

Part 2

Write an answer to **one** of the questions **2–4** in this part. Write your answer in **220–260** words in an appropriate style.

---

2   You read this extract from an article in an English-language newspaper:

> It is becoming more and more unusual these days to see children playing outside on bikes or kicking a football around. The popularity of the Internet and computer games is having a negative effect on children's health, fitness and social skills.

You decide to write a letter to the Editor of the newspaper explaining your views on the points raised in the article and giving reasons for your opinions.

Write your **letter**.

3   You see the following announcement on a music website:

> ### Music Festivals
>
> Some music festivals provide great entertainment for the whole family, while others are aimed at particular groups of people. We're looking for reviews from you, our readers, about a music festival you've been to.
>
> Tell us how memorable you think the festival was for its audience and make suggestions for how it could be improved in future. We'll publish the best reviews on our website.

Write your **review**.

4   You attend a college that has many international students. You feel that the college website does not do enough to support new international students. You decide to write a proposal to the College Principal, explaining how the college website could be improved to help these students.

In your proposal, outline what extra information or advice you would include on the website, and explain how this might help international students make the most of their time at the college.

Write your **proposal**.

LISTENING (approximately 40 minutes)

Part 1

You will hear three different extracts. For questions **1–6**, choose the answer (**A**, **B** or **C**) which fits best according to what you hear. There are two questions for each extract.

Extract One

You hear a man telling a friend about his holiday.

1 The man thinks the essential component of a holiday is

   A physical activity.

   B the opportunity to travel.

   C mental stimulation.

2 He feels that one benefit of doing archaeology on holiday is that it

   A provides him with the excitement of discovery.

   B adds to the sum of his knowledge.

   C helps him to be more tolerant.

Extract Two

You hear two colleagues talking about time management.

3 They agree that being late

   A is a growing trend.

   B is a difficult habit to break.

   C can be amusing when it affects others.

4 In the woman's opinion, people who fail to arrive on time

   A are often completely unaware of the problems they cause.

   B generally have a relaxed attitude to life.

   C are putting their career prospects at risk.

Extract Three

You hear two friends talking about a historical novel they have read.

5   The woman thinks the novelist manages to

    A   create a credible background.

    B   exploit a strong story line.

    C   depict well-drawn characters.

6   The friends agree that this historical novel

    A   gives a successful insight into the past.

    B   provides an escape from the present.

    C   presents a highly subjective view of events.

Part 2

You will hear a photographer and TV cameraman called Mike Darby talking about his life and work. For questions **7–14**, complete the sentences with a word or short phrase.

PHOTOGRAPHER AND CAMERAMAN

Mike says that among his older colleagues, **(7)** ....

rather than photography, was a common degree subject.

While working as a diver at a **(8)** .... in the Antarctic, Mike decided to

become a photographer.

Mike feels that an aptitude for **(9)** .... is the key business skill in his work.

Mike's most recent shoot involved taking pictures for a **(10)** ....

Mike is proudest of the book called **(11)** ....

In his most recent TV work as a wildlife cameraman Mike filmed different types of

(12) .... in various locations.

Mike uses the word **(13)** ....

to emphasise how his work as a cameraman differs from his book projects.

Mike advises young photographers to invent **(14)** ....

to go with their pictures when they try to sell them.

Part 3

You will hear part of an interview in which two experts called Kirsten Neet and Anton Best are discussing the idea of what's called 'information overload'. For questions **15–20**, choose the answer (**A**, **B**, **C** or **D**) which fits best according to what you hear.

---

15 What aspect of modern life does Anton think Seneca anticipated?

   A The fact that intellectuals sometimes reject new ideas.
   B The fact that an interest in owning books has decreased.
   C The way that people get distracted by passing trends.
   D The way that people have become obsessed with the notion of quality.

16 In Kirsten's view, the volume of material available today

   A makes us too reliant on technology.
   B is far less useful than we think it might be.
   C is not significantly greater than in the past.
   D presents a problem which has always existed.

17 How does Anton respond to the suggestion of doing without much of today's information?

   A He feels it might actually lead to meaningful progress.
   B He says it would be betraying the past.
   C He thinks the solution lies in technological systems.
   D He would prefer to see a reduction in the quantity produced.

18 In discussing the problem of dealing with information overload today, the two experts agree that

   A it is reaching a critical point.
   B the methods used are ineffective.
   C it makes people communicate less.
   D the concept of convenience has been lost.

19 Kirsten sees the biggest work-related benefit arising from greater available information as

   A the rapid advances in direct feedback.
   B the spread of personalised advertising.
   C more worker participation in product development.
   D a marked increase in customer satisfaction.

20 What does Kirsten say dieting made her realise about information?

   A restrict your own access to it
   B only a small part of it is ever accurate
   C only bother with it when you really have to
   D be highly selective when faced with a lot of it

Test 2

Part 4

You will hear five short extracts in which people are talking about a course they did in business administration.

TASK ONE

For questions **21–25**, choose from the list (**A–H**) each speaker's main reason for doing the course.

TASK TWO

For questions **26–30**, choose from the list (**A–H**) what each speaker gained as a result of doing the course.

While you listen you must complete both tasks.

A	to improve promotion prospects	

B	to explore a new subject	Speaker 1	21
C	to keep up with developments in a field	Speaker 2	22
D	to enhance existing abilities	Speaker 3	23
E	to impress a current employer	Speaker 4	24
F	to find effective ways to support others	Speaker 5	25
G	to discover how to succeed independently		
H	to increase the possibilities of employment		

A	the fulfilment of a long-term ambition		
B	a high-powered job in another country	Speaker 1	26
C	significant financial rewards	Speaker 2	27
D	a prestigious managerial appointment	Speaker 3	28
E	the chance to gain a foothold in business	Speaker 4	29
F	the creation of a new company	Speaker 5	30
G	a period of re-adjustment		
H	the development of a specific product		

SPEAKING (15 minutes)

There are two examiners. One (the interlocutor) conducts the test, providing you with the necessary materials and explaining what you have to do. The other examiner (the assessor) is introduced to you, but then takes no further part in the interaction.

Part 1 (2 minutes)

The interlocutor first asks you and your partner a few questions. The interlocutor asks candidates for some information about themselves, then widens the scope of the questions by asking about e.g. candidates' leisure activities, studies, travel and daily life. Candidates are expected to respond to the interlocutor's questions and listen to what their partner has to say.

Part 2 (a one-minute 'long turn' for each candidate, plus a 30-second response from the second candidate)

You are each given the opportunity to talk for about a minute, and to comment briefly after your partner has spoken.

The interlocutor gives you a set of pictures and asks you to talk about them for about one minute. It is important to listen carefully to the interlocutor's instructions. The interlocutor then asks your partner a question about your pictures and your partner responds briefly.

You are then given another set of pictures to look at. Your partner talks about these pictures for about one minute. This time the interlocutor asks you a question about your partner's pictures and you respond briefly.

Part 3 (4 minutes)

In this part of the test, you and your partner are asked to talk together. The interlocutor places some text prompts on the table between you. This stimulus provides the basis for a discussion. The interlocutor explains what you have to do.

Part 4 (5 minutes)

The interlocutor asks some further questions, which leads to a more general discussion of what you have talked about in Part 3. You may comment on your partner's answers if you wish.

Test 3

READING AND USE OF ENGLISH (1 hour 30 minutes)

Part 1

For questions **1–8**, read the text below and decide which answer (**A**, **B**, **C** or **D**) best fits each gap.
There is an example at the beginning (**0**).
Mark your answers **on the separate answer sheet**.

Example:

0 A aspect   **B** part   **C** element   **D** factor

0	A	B	C	D
	☐	■	☐	☐

The Japanese Bobtail

Cats have been **(0)** …….. of the lives of human beings for thousands of years. One interesting breed which fascinates scientists is the Japanese Bobtail – a domestic cat with an unusual 'bobbed' tail more **(1)** …….. resembling the tail of a rabbit than that of other cats. The breed has been known in Japan for centuries, and it features **(2)** …….. in folklore. In many traditions, cats are frequently **(3)** …….. of fear and mistrust but in Japanese stories the Bobtail tends to be **(4)** …….. as a force for **(5)** …….. . The image of a Bobtail seated with one paw raised is considered a lucky charm.

But how did the Bobtail **(6)** …….. its short tail? One legend tells of a sleeping cat whose long tail **(7)** …….. fire. In a panic, it tore through the town, spreading flames everywhere. As a result, the then emperor declared that all cats should have their tails cut short as a **(8)** …….. measure. Science, however, has a less 'romantic' explanation based on genetics.

1	**A**	nearly	**B**	similarly	**C**	accurately	**D**	closely
2	**A**	prominently	**B**	obviously	**C**	appreciably	**D**	significantly
3	**A**	products	**B**	articles	**C**	objects	**D**	elements
4	**A**	assumed	**B**	portrayed	**C**	exposed	**D**	disclosed
5	**A**	right	**B**	virtue	**C**	good	**D**	truth
6	**A**	come by	**B**	get at	**C**	hit on	**D**	go for
7	**A**	took	**B**	caught	**C**	set	**D**	seized
8	**A**	defensive	**B**	restrictive	**C**	preventative	**D**	corrective

Part 2

For questions **9–16**, read the text below and think of the word which best fits each gap. Use only **one** word in each gap. There is an example at the beginning (**0**).

Write your answers **IN CAPITAL LETTERS on the separate answer sheet**.

Example: | 0 | | O | F | | | | | | | | | | | | | | | |

Work experience abroad

Every year thousands **(0)** …….. young people in various countries do short periods of work in

other countries **(9)** …….. the time they leave school and start university. Typically these involve

helping in schools or hospitals, or on conservation projects. The experience the young people gain

will be of great benefit in their lives. **(10)** …….. a personal point of view, it gives them a sense of

independence and confidence. It may also help them with their long-term career.

There are many organisations that run work experience programmes. **(11)** …….. such company

is Global Volunteers, **(12)** …….. spokesperson Mary Cooper comments: '**(13)** …….. than being

an extended holiday, our placements involve learning to **(14)** …….. responsibility for themselves.

Young people should push themselves out of their comfort zones and do **(15)** …….. productive.

Doing a placement will add value to a CV, helping young people to **(16)** …….. out from the crowd

in the job market. Some employers look favourably on students who have the initiative and drive

to complete one.'

Part 3

For questions **17–24**, read the text below. Use the word given in capitals at the end of some of the lines to form a word that fits in the gap **in the same line**. There is an example at the beginning (**0**).

Write your answers **IN CAPITAL LETTERS on the separate answer sheet**.

Example:

0	A	D	A	P	T	A	B	L	E								

The significance of hairstyles

Hair is the most easily (**0**) …….. part of the human body and also one of   **ADAPT** able

the most (**17**) …….. . The first barbers appeared in ancient Greece, when   **DISTINCT** ive

short hair became a sign of social status. Similarly, South American Inca

chiefs had their hair short; in contrast, the hair of their citizens got (**18**) ……..   **PROGRESS** ively

longer the further down the social chain they were. Barbers prospered in the

days of the Roman Empire, until they were expelled from Rome, when it was

discovered how much they earned.

Women have always reflected fashion through their hairstyles, sometimes

quite (**19**) …….. . In 15th-century Europe, women would pluck the hair from   **DRAMA** TICALLY

the front of their heads in (**20**) …….. of beauty. Three centuries later, the   **PURSUE**

fashion was for huge hairstyles that made it (**21**) …….. for the hairdresser   **NEED**

to climb a small ladder. The maintenance needed to (**22**) …….. these styles   **SURE**

looked good was enormous. Today, in our more liberal world, very little

is socially (**23**) …….. with regard to hairstyles and technology has been   **ACCEPT** UNACCEPT

enormously (**24**) …….. in reducing the time we spend on our hair.   **BENEFIT** IAL

Part 4

For questions **25–30**, complete the second sentence so that it has a similar meaning to the first sentence, using the word given. **Do not change the word given.** You must use between **three** and **six** words, including the word given. Here is an example (**0**).

Example:

0 James would only speak to the head of department alone.

    ON

    James ………………………………… to the head of department alone.

The gap can be filled with the words 'insisted on speaking', so you write:

Example:	**0**	INSISTED ON SPEAKING

Write **only** the missing words **IN CAPITAL LETTERS on the separate answer sheet**.

---

25 The constant public attention on famous people must have an effect on them.

    EYE

    Constantly ………………………………….. must have an effect on famous people.

26 This building would be ideal for our new office except that there are no parking facilities nearby.

    FROM

    apart from the lack of

    This building would be ideal for our new office ………………………………….. of parking facilities nearby.

27 It's only because of the quality of the lead singer's voice that people listen to the album.

    WORTH

    made e sit the album worth

    It's the quality of the lead singer's voice that ………………………………….. to.

28 The hotel wasn't just far from the sea, it was expensive too.

ONLY

Not ……………………….……... way from the sea, it was expensive too.

29 Jenny felt she had stayed too long at the party.

HIGH

Jenny felt it ………………………….…... the party.

30 Hannah's essay doesn't have a clear enough explanation of the main point to be awarded top marks.

CLEARLY

Hannah's essay doesn't …………………………….…... to be awarded top marks.

Part 5

You are going to read a newspaper article about research into a chemical. For questions **31–36**, choose the answer (**A**, **B**, **C** or **D**) which you think fits best according to the text.
Mark your answers **on the separate answer sheet**.

Oxytocin

Oliver Burkeman asks the US academic Paul Zak about his research into a chemical called oxytocin, which has an important role in our lives.

Paul Zak is renowned among his colleagues for two things he does disconcertingly soon after meeting people. The first is hugging: seeing me approach, he springs to his feet, and enfolds me in his arms. The second is talking them into having needles stuck into their arms to draw blood. I escape our encounter unpunctured, but plenty don't – willingly, of course. Zak's work has involved extracting blood from, amongst others, a couple on their wedding day, people who have been dancing, and a group in Papua New Guinea preparing to perform traditional rituals.

Having dipped into his book, *The Moral Molecule*, I know that what drives Zak's hunger for blood is his interest in oxytocin. Long known as a female reproductive hormone, oxytocin emerges from Zak's research as something much more. Being treated decently, he says, causes people's oxytocin levels to rise, prompting them to behave more decently, while experimental subjects given an artificial oxytocin boost behave more generously and trustingly. Describing the chemical as the 'moral molecule that keeps society together', Zak offers nothing less than a vast explanation of whole swathes of philosophical questions. The subtitle of the book, *the new science of what makes us good or evil*, gives a sense of this.

line 16 The aforementioned wedding took place at a house in England, where Zak set up the equipment needed to collect blood. He took samples, before and after the ceremony, from the bride and groom, and various guests, then transferred his spoils to his laboratory. There, he discovered the results he'd been expecting: the ceremony caused oxytocin to spike. And it did so 'in direct proportion to the likely intensity of emotional engagement in the event'.

The bride recorded the highest increase, followed by close family members, then less closely involved friends. Mapping the wedding's oxytocin levels gave rise, in Zak's words, to an amazing human 'solar system' with the bride as the sun, the hormone finely calibrated to the emotional warmth each guest felt.

Zak's interest in oxytocin was fuelled by experiments involving the Trust Game. Participant A is invited to lend some money to a stranger, Participant B. They're told that any money A sends will triple in value, whereupon B can return some as a thank-you. According to traditional models, the game should break down before it begins. B, acting selfishly, has no reason to give any money back – and, knowing this, A shouldn't send any in the first place. However, as in previous research with this tried and tested set up, the vast majority of A-people send money, while an even larger percentage of B-people return some. Zak's analysis of the oxytocin in participants' bloodstreams reveals that by sending money to B, person A is giving a sign of trust – and for person B, being on the receiving end causes oxytocin levels to increase, motivating more generous behaviour in return.

The possible implications are intriguing. Evolution has given us oxytocin, a biological mechanism that lets us be instinctively trusting and kind – or 'moral'. Mixing science and morality prompts suspicion, however. Just because something is 'natural' doesn't mean it's 'right', and efforts to derive moral codes from science rarely end well. Moreover, it's unclear what Zak means when he says oxytocin, or the lack of it, 'makes' us good or evil. Still, none of this undermines the pragmatic aspect of Zak's work. If oxytocin is the mechanism through which moral action takes place, then by manipulating oxytocin, we might boost levels of trust, generosity, and ultimately happiness.

On the other hand, what's to stop car dealers, say, pumping oxytocin into showrooms? Zak waves the matter away: it's incredibly hard to get enough oxytocin into the bloodstream. Sure, oxytocin can be stimulated in subtle ways to serve other people's agendas, 'but they're already doing that. Why do you think they have babies in adverts? To make you feel good, by provoking the release of oxytocin.' Meanwhile, he says, we should all do at least eight hugs a day, massage and even watch soppy movies – he's done the tests. Interaction on social media seems to lead to oxytocin spikes, undermining the argument that it's killing real human interaction; hormonally, it appears, the body processes it as real interaction.

31   What does the writer suggest about Paul Zak in the first paragraph?

   A   He provokes mixed feelings in people.
   B   He understands that aggression can sometimes be useful.
   C   He can adapt himself to a variety of situations.
   D   He is capable of being very persuasive.

32   What does 'spoils' refer to in line 16?

   A   equipment
   B   samples
   C   guests
   D   results

33   What is the writer's purpose in the fourth paragraph?

   A   to make a counter-argument
   B   to introduce a new concept
   C   to summarise an idea
   D   to expand on a point

34   What does the writer say about Zak's Trust Game experiments?

   A   They demonstrate the importance of money in human relations.
   B   Their artificiality means that what they tell us is of limited value.
   C   The results challenge conventional notions of human behaviour.
   D   They were constructed in a way that was clever and innovative.

35   What does the writer suggest in the sixth paragraph?

   A   The potential exploitation of oxytocin should be given serious consideration.
   B   Zak's experimental methods are the object of some mistrust.
   C   Further work is needed to define exactly what oxytocin is.
   D   Science cannot be free of ethical considerations.

36   How does Zak regard the idea of deliberately manipulating oxytocin?

   A   He doubts whether it's ever going to be feasible.
   B   He worries about possible commercial misuse.
   C   He advocates wider use of readily available means.
   D   He feels it's outside his area of expertise.

Part 6

You are going to read four extracts from online articles about childhood. For questions **37–40**, choose from the extracts **A–D**. The extracts may be chosen more than once.

Mark your answers **on the separate answer sheet**.

The Changing Face of Childhood in the USA

A   Mary Granger
Parents often complain that childhood today seems different to what it was when they were young – when a free day meant they ran care-free out the door after breakfast and played until twilight. But they are somewhat hypocritical, because many of today's better-off children seem to have less time for such unstructured play as they face an unfortunate mass of parent-organised 'things-to-keep-kids-busy' that might include karate lessons, tutoring or ballet. Parents are increasingly unwilling to let their offspring play outside. As a result children are more protected than ever before. A generation ago children went cycling on their own, went on public transport alone, took responsibility for themselves. Some experts suggest that the whole nature of parenting was different; that it was much less hands-on and more trusting of the child.

B   Max Poenbaum
The interaction between the child and the natural environment provides an authentic learning experience based on sensory absorption and investigation, but it disappears with the passing of childhood. Then adult cognitive reasoning gradually takes over as the world is seen in a more objective or scientific way. At the transition between childhood and adulthood, young people can feel in danger of having nothing stable to hold on to, caught between the trapeze of childhood that has been let go of and the trapeze of growing up not yet within his or her grasp. Now parents must become a safety net at a time when the young person feels naturally anxious and insecure. But these days, parents are struggling against the slow creep of an increasingly commercial and sexualised culture and behaviour. That very culture, which is so rightly blamed for preventing younger children from being children also undermines the parenting of teenagers.

C   John P. Ondorenko
It is clear that young children have a special affinity for the great outdoors that is connected to their development and their ways of knowing and learning. This is a unique and unrepeatable ability that starts to fade during the teenage years. Even so, today's teenagers are under pressure to grow up before they are ready. Celebrity culture, adult-style clothes and music videos are all guilty of encouraging them to act older than they are. As a result they are adrift in a sea of disaffection. In particular they care less about school performance and social obedience than ever before. On the flip side, they are much more tolerant and aware of ethical issues and also more caring regarding the future of the planet. A common adolescent complaint is of ever-increasing boredom, and yet children today have no reason to be bored, partly as the number of formal, extra-curricular activities available to them is unprecedented.

D   Steven Zafaria
Once the pre-teen years are gone, parents have a more aloof adolescent who is more reluctant to be touched, who would rather spend time with friends, who feels too old to play with parents, who is embarrassed by their public company, who is more private and less forthcoming, and who seems to court their disapproval through deliberate resistance and opposition. The pattern is a standard one and always has been, as any psychologist will tell you. Teenagers may think they are fully independent, fiercely so in fact, but parents must be there for them, taking a back seat, intervening less than before, but ready to listen and guide when called upon. But parenting is becoming increasingly complex. The increasingly commercialised and sexualised world we live in means that children are missing out on a proper childhood. The solution is clearly not to keep children wholly innocent until they are adults, but we have surely reached the point where some regulatory protection is required.

Which expert

has a similar view to Poenbaum on how long people's instinctive relationship with nature lasts? `37`

expresses a similar opinion to Zafaria on what the role of a parent should be regarding teenage children? `38`

has a different view from the others on whether children are growing up too fast? `39`

expresses a different opinion from Ondorenko on the value of planned activities for children? `40`

Part 7

You are going to read an extract from a newspaper article about travelling in Poland. Six paragraphs have been removed from the extract. Choose from the paragraphs **A–G** the one which fits each gap (**41–46**). There is one extra paragraph which you do not need to use.
Mark your answers **on the separate answer sheet.**

Before Google ... the alternative travel guide to Poland

Vicky Baker takes social networking back to its roots by resurrecting a travel project in Poland from the early 1990s.

'I am going to take you to my friend's studio. It's quite unusual,' says Jarek, my unofficial guide to Kraków, in one of the biggest understatements of the trip. He leads me to an old cottage. It looks abandoned, but then we are greeted by a man who, with his grey beard and sheepskin waistcoat, looks like an ageing pop star. Outside there's a two-metre-high carved totem pole and the remains of a bonfire are still burning.

41

As a couch surfer I am used to finding golden opportunities through strangers, but the unusual thing about this connection is that it came about after I tried to reconstruct a tourism project that was, in many ways, the precursor to modern social networking. Back in the 1980s, US-born Jim Haynes, a renowned supporter of alternative arts, had an idea. Convinced that the best travel experiences come from the people you meet, he set himself a goal: he would match inquisitive travellers with gracious hosts by creating an alternative guidebook, in a country he loved. *Poland: People to People* finally hit the bookshelves in 1991.

42

Eventually enough people came forward with their contact details and a willingness to participate in the scheme. Jim assembled all the names in what read like a personal address book. The cover price of £6 bought you the contact details of 1,000 strangers.

43

Intrigued by the idea of taking modern networking back to its roots, I wondered whether, many years later, Jim's hosts would still be willing to greet an unknown visitor from overseas. But first I would have to track them down.

44

At first I planned to communicate only by post and sent several letters before realising I lacked the patience. Feeling a little guilty, I opted for the 21st-century solution: searching for the names on the Internet. Many were dead ends; others simply never responded. But gradually people did come forward and I received various slightly stunned replies. Before long I had meetings arranged in Kraków and Gdansk.

45

I skip the organised tours, though, and head off to meet Wladek, a 50-year-old academic. We meet in a 19th-century café, where an ultra-polite waitress sets down a massive plate of Polish dumplings before us. It is too much for any tourist to eat.

46

I'm charmed by Kraków and reluctant to leave Wladek, who proves to be excellent company, and the café, but I already have my next meeting arranged a 10-hour train ride away. Gdansk, with its immaculately renovated buildings and little boutiques, is clearly a world away from the city it was in the 1990s. I have arranged to meet kite-surfing enthusiast Mariusz at a restaurant there. *Poland: People to People* lives on, it seems. I know Jim will be delighted.

A Peer to peer websites are common now, but turning the idea into a book back then was a challenge. Jim sent out hundreds of letters through his already extensive network of friends and placed small ads in various Polish publications.

B My new acquaintance has hazy memories of the people he met through the book, but says he enjoys the company of visitors, as they are curious and interested in others. He shows me old photos and speaks of how life has changed here.

C What follows is one of those surreal travel experiences, where one new friend introduces you to another and another. Before long we've set off on a tour of Kraków's artistic community.

D That was easier said than done. Details were sparse; just contact details and a very short profile. 'I live in Kraków and I am a man of Kraków,' read one rather unhelpful entry.

E Jim gave me an out-of-print edition at one of the open-house dinners he runs every Sunday at his Paris home. It was like opening a little time capsule and from that moment I knew what I had to do.

F The next morning is the occasion of my impromptu adventure with Jarek, an artist I found after contacting various local galleries. He invites me for dinner and even finds the original typewritten letter Jim sent in 1989 to introduce the project.

G It is my first time in Poland, and the former is undeniably impressive. The picture-perfect main square is lined with Renaissance buildings, lively street cafés and golf carts waiting to take tourists around town.

Part 8

You are going to read four book reviews. For questions **47–56**, choose from the sections (**A–D**). The sections may be chosen more than once.

Mark your answers **on the separate answer sheet**.

Of which book are the following stated?

It presents complicated material in manageable chunks of data.	47	B
The book failed to sustain the reviewer's interest throughout.	48	A
Readers are left to draw their own conclusions about some of the book's material.	49	C
Its author sought expert advice on certain aspects of the book.	50	
The book is both instructive and visually appealing.	51	D
It looks both backwards and forwards in time.	52	A
Its author effectively brings together different fields of study.	53	
It offers a selective, rather than comprehensive, coverage of its topic.	54	
It is possible to feel a sense of involvement with the subject matter.	55	
The text is a skilful mixture of data and personal comment.	56	

NATURE BOOKS

A WHY ELEPHANTS HAVE BIG EARS by Chris Lavers

Chris Lavers has set out to produce a book that sits neatly between serious scholarship (he is a senior lecturer in animal ecology) and the need to satisfy the inquisitive pesterings of children. Why are ants so small? Why can a bat fly and a shrew not? And of course, why do elephants have big ears? The answer is no shocker – creatures have interacted with their habitats to evolve into the extraordinary forms they possess today. But once this principle is established, the book loses some of its charm. The book's most successful sections are where we travel through the Jurassic and Cretaceous periods of prehistory to look at how nature made its primal decisions: which species would fly and which would swim, which creatures would be warm or cold-blooded? Lavers argues that it is here we find the true answers to our questions today and the principles to safely predict our future.

B ORIGINS: The Evolution of Continents, Oceans and Life by Ron Redfern

Shortlisted for the BP Natural World Book Prize, *Origins* comprises panoramas and a wide-ranging, accessible scientific insight to make this work a fresh interpretation of the Earth's fascinating evolution. The landscape photographs were shot specifically for the book, albeit by the author himself, after consultation with leading scientists to find the location of the best-known examples of various forms and processes. The writer manages to reduce the most complex theories to digestible nuggets of information. The text is an entertaining narrative that successfully weaves recent and ancient history with science. *Origins* is a heavyweight work in more ways than one: as a test for the legs of any coffee table and as a definitive guide to our planet's evolution. It is ideal for regular dipping into as much as for in-depth reference.

C EARTH ODYSSEY by Mark Hertsgaard

Worried about the effects of our expanding population on the world's resources, Mark Hertsgaard took a world tour to see for himself how bad things really were. *Earth Odyssey* is the culmination of seven years' work, during which time he visited 19 countries. To read it is to shadow him on his tour and to observe the condition of the planet through the eyes of the people he met along the way: their living conditions, their personal struggles and triumphs. He does not try to offer his own opinions; rather he lets us make our own minds up. Hertsgaard cleverly interweaves his observations with carefully gathered evidence as he seeks to answer questions about our environment. He takes us through the industrial and agricultural revolutions, then back to the origins of the human species, to see if the past can provide any answers. Although the answers we want to hear sit uneasily with the facts, Hertsgaard presents an elegant portrait of the human species, full of character, dignity, perseverance and strength. He leaves you with a strong conviction that it is ultimately a race worth saving.

D THE VIKING ATLAS OF EVOLUTION by Roger Osbourne

Why are there no penguins in the Arctic, or polar bears in Antarctica? How is it that camels and llamas are so closely related, yet they live so far apart? The answers come down to the fact that evolution takes place according to geographical location as well as time. Using photographs, superb illustrations and more than 100 maps showing distributions of organisms, migrations, territories and biogeographic regions, the atlas graphically highlights the impact geography has had on the development of life on Earth. It charts the origins, evolution and spread of plants, reptiles, birds and mammals worldwide. It also investigates the way people have altered the world they live in, from the introduction of exotic species into fragile ecosystems to the destruction of habitats and the domestication of wild species. The accompanying text is highly informative. The atlas does not review the evolution of every 'important' life form on the planet. Rather, it chooses several case studies to highlight the evolutionary process in differing geographical settings.

WRITING (1 hour 30 minutes)

Part 1

You **must** answer this question. Write your answer in **220–260** words in an appropriate style.

---

1 You have listened to a radio discussion programme about how to motivate children to do regular exercise. You have made the notes below:

Ways of motivating children to do regular exercise:
- parental example
- government funding
- school

Some opinions expressed in the discussion:

"If children don't see their parents do exercise, they don't think it's important."

"If sports facilities were cheaper, more people would use them."

"Sport in schools is too competitive. It should be fun for everyone."

Write an essay for your tutor discussing **two** of the ways in your notes. You should **explain which way is more effective** in motivating children to do regular exercise and **provide reasons** to support your opinion.

You may, if you wish, make use of the opinions expressed in the discussion, but you should use your own words as far as possible.

Part 2

Write an answer to **one** of the questions **2–4** in this part. Write your answer in **220–260** words in an appropriate style.

---

2   You are studying at an international college and you recently attended a careers day organised by the college to help students prepare for work. The event included information about how to identify suitable jobs, workshops on writing effective job applications, and advice on how to do well in interviews.

The College Principal has asked you to write a report evaluating to what extent the event was successful and making recommendations for next year's event.

Write your **report**.

3   You receive this letter from a friend who is planning to study abroad:

> I'm not sure about going to study abroad anymore. How will I meet people and find somewhere to live? And I'm worried I won't understand my lessons. Maybe it's not the right thing for me after all!

You decide to write to your friend giving your opinion and offering advice.

Write your **letter**.

4   You see the following announcement on a travel website:

> ## Outdoor Activity Holidays
>
> If you've been on an outdoor activity holiday then we'd love to hear from you. Maybe you went horse riding, rock climbing or windsurfing, for example. Write a review for our website evaluating the location, facilities and activities, and explaining why you would, or wouldn't, recommend it to other holidaymakers.

Write your **review**.

LISTENING (approximately 40 minutes)

Part 1

You will hear three different extracts. For questions **1–6**, choose the answer (**A**, **B** or **C**) which fits best according to what you hear. There are two questions for each extract.

Extract One

You hear two people discussing climate change.

1   How did the man feel after watching a TV debate on the subject?

    A   alarmed by the strength of feeling among the speakers

    B   dismayed by some of the speakers' level of knowledge

    C   surprised by the number of speakers taking part

2   The woman thinks that articles about climate change should

    A   be written by scientists.

    B   include some humour.

    C   be authenticated by specialists.

Extract Two

You hear two pilots taking part in a discussion programme about an aerobatics team in which they fly.

3   How does the man feel about the new training season?

    A   concerned about his ability to learn new skills

    B   satisfied that his efforts have been worthwhile

    C   worried about the number of hours he has to put in

4   What does the woman think about the forthcoming world championships?

    A   She has confidence in the ability of certain team members.

    B   She's convinced that the team will do better than last year.

    C   She suspects that pilots have been given unrealistic targets.

Extract Three

You hear two friends talking about online book reviews.

5   The woman reveals her belief that

   A   websites should monitor contributions.

   B   reading such reviews is a waste of time.

   C   those who write reviews are unscrupulous.

6   How does the man think he benefits from writing online reviews?

   A   It allows him to share his opinions.

   B   It gives him practice in writing skills.

   C   It makes him read the books more closely.

Part 2

You will hear a student, called Greg Pritchard, talking about his gap year trip to Africa.
For questions **7–14**, complete the sentences with a word or short phrase.

GAP YEAR TRIP

Greg says that the Kruger National Park is home to the largest population of

| | **7** | in South Africa.

Greg was surprised that so many people chose to study

| | **8** | during the first week of the trip.

On Greg's research project, he was responsible for recording the

| | **9** | of the crocodiles sighted.

Greg learned that | | **10** | will be fitted to some large crocodiles

in future.

Greg was pleased that he managed to find some | | **11** | to eat

when he went on a wilderness trail.

Greg describes himself as becoming more | | **12** | during the third

week of his trip.

During the fourth week of his trip, Greg taught | | **13** | in a

village school.

Greg thinks that sharing | | **14** | with local villagers taught him

most about their culture.

Part 3

You will hear part of an interview with two board game enthusiasts called Sarah Walters and Ed Zander about the renewed popularity of traditional board games. For questions **15–20**, choose the answer (**A**, **B**, **C** or **D**) which fits best according to what you hear.

---

15   Sarah thinks board games are becoming more popular partly

      A   as a consequence of their basic simplicity.
      B   as a reaction to the dominance of technology.
      C   because they mirror already popular gaming activities.
      D   because people are constantly searching for new hobbies.

16   Ed thinks game playing will grow in this century

      A   as a result of people having more leisure time.
      B   as a way of enhancing personal relationships.
      C   as a means of coping with increasingly stressful lives.
      D   as a reflection of fundamental changes taking place in society.

17   In Sarah's opinion, what is the main attraction of board games?

      A   the challenges they pose to players
      B   the memories they evoke of the past
      C   the environment in which they take place
      D   the competitive element in the way they are played

18   When asked if board-gaming is a world-wide phenomenon, Ed

      A   explains a trend which is likely to change.
      B   highlights the importance of advertising and marketing.
      C   mentions the huge variety of games available globally.
      D   emphasises the differences that exist between parts of the world.

19   Sarah sees the Game of the Year award as

      A   a useful marketing tool.
      B   crucial as a way of promoting variety.
      C   important in keeping consumers informed.
      D   a positive development for younger players.

20   When talking about their own collections of board games, Ed and Sarah agree that

      A   some are likely to prove an investment.
      B   many are beautifully manufactured.
      C   collectors sometimes regret their purchases.
      D   throwing games away isn't advisable.

Part 4

You will hear five short extracts in which people are talking about having more than one job at a time.

TASK ONE

For questions **21–25**, choose from the list (**A–H**) why each speaker took on more than one job.

TASK TWO

For questions **26–30**, choose from the list (**A–H**) the unexpected result of having more than one job that each speaker refers to.

While you listen you must complete both tasks.

A to avoid potential monotony	**A** becoming well-known locally
B to widen useful contacts	**B** working with a famous name
C to pay for accommodation	**C** receiving a special assignment
D to enhance promotion prospects	**D** starting a personal relationship
E to leave a dull workplace	**E** creating a new fashion
F to find a sense of satisfaction	**F** getting professional recognition
G to seek a different direction	**G** achieving true celebrity status
H to achieve a long-held ambition	**H** running a successful business

Speaker 1	**21**	Speaker 1	**26**
Speaker 2	**22**	Speaker 2	**27**
Speaker 3	**23**	Speaker 3	**28**
Speaker 4	**24**	Speaker 4	**29**
Speaker 5	**25**	Speaker 5	**30**

SPEAKING (15 minutes)

There are two examiners. One (the interlocutor) conducts the test, providing you with the necessary materials and explaining what you have to do. The other examiner (the assessor) is introduced to you, but then takes no further part in the interaction.

Part 1 (2 minutes)

The interlocutor first asks you and your partner a few questions. The interlocutor asks candidates for some information about themselves, then widens the scope of the questions by asking about e.g. candidates' leisure activities, studies, travel and daily life. Candidates are expected to respond to the interlocutor's questions and listen to what their partner has to say.

Part 2 (a one-minute 'long turn' for each candidate, plus a 30-second response from the second candidate)

You are each given the opportunity to talk for about a minute, and to comment briefly after your partner has spoken.

The interlocutor gives you a set of pictures and asks you to talk about them for about one minute. It is important to listen carefully to the interlocutor's instructions. The interlocutor then asks your partner a question about your pictures and your partner responds briefly.

You are then given another set of pictures to look at. Your partner talks about these pictures for about one minute. This time the interlocutor asks you a question about your partner's pictures and you respond briefly.

Part 3 (4 minutes)

In this part of the test, you and your partner are asked to talk together. The interlocutor places some text prompts on the table between you. This stimulus provides the basis for a discussion. The interlocutor explains what you have to do.

Part 4 (5 minutes)

The interlocutor asks some further questions, which leads to a more general discussion of what you have talked about in Part 3. You may comment on your partner's answers if you wish.

Test 4

READING AND USE OF ENGLISH (1 hour 30 minutes)

Part 1

For questions **1–8**, read the text below and decide which answer (**A**, **B**, **C** or **D**) best fits each gap. There is an example at the beginning (**0**).

Mark your answers **on the separate answer sheet**.

Example:

0 A assessment   **B** account   **C** expression   **D** estimate

0	A	B	C	D
	☐	☐	▬	☐

Dressing for success

Whether you like it or not, when you go for a job interview your personal appearance will be judged as an **(0)** .... of who you are. Just from looking at you, the interviewer will start **(1)** .... an opinion about your capabilities, your attitude to work and how well you might **(2)** .... their organisation. The right image is one that helps the interviewer **(3)** .... you as one of their team and **(4)** .... them that you could represent their company. So, find out about the company dress code prior to the interview, or see how people are dressed on their corporate website.

However, even if you **(5)** .... the image right, it may not **(6)** .... be remarked on. The interviewer will just sense that you 'look right', and feel **(7)** .... to being convinced that you are the right person for the job. But if you get it wrong, it can be very difficult to **(8)** .... the negative impression you may already have made.

1 **A** shaping   **B** making   **C** creating   **D** forming

2 **A** put up with   **B** settle down to **C** fit in with   **D** live up to

3 **A** visualise   **B** reflect   **C** observe   **D** foresee

4 **A** reassures   **B** clarifies   **C** encourages   **D** supports

5 **A** put   **B** get   **C** hit   **D** set

6 **A** significantly **B** necessarily   **C** appropriately **D** strictly

7 **A** open   **B** free   **C** alert   **D** aware

8 **A** overtake   **B** overthrow   **C** overdo   **D** overcome

Part 2

For questions **9–16**, read the text below and think of the word which best fits each gap. Use only **one** word in each gap. There is an example at the beginning (**0**).

Write your answers **IN CAPITAL LETTERS on the separate answer sheet**.

Example: | **0** | | N | O | T | | | | | | | | | | | | | | | | |

How technology is helping people to talk

The term 'eye-gaze technology' may **(0)** …….. mean much to most people, but it can be life-changing for anyone suffering from a severe speech problem. **(9)** …….. been invited to try one such hi-tech communication aid, I find **(10)** …….. sitting staring at a computer screen. As a journalist, this is nothing new for me **(11)** …….. for the fact that this screen features a red dot which tracks the movement of my eyes.

I start by looking at a letter from an on-screen keyboard. However, I could, **(12)** …….. I wanted to, select alternative screens **(13)** …….. up of vocabulary and expressions, which, for experienced users, would **(14)** …….. doubt speed things up. The letter or word I've selected pops up at the top of the screen, and slowly I build up my message. More speed would be good as this isn't a fast way to communicate, **(15)** …….. with the aid of predictive text. After **(16)** …….. seems like a long time, my phrase 'this is an amazing machine' is complete. I stare at the phrase and it comes back to me in a synthesised voice.

Part 3

For questions **17–24**, read the text below. Use the word given in capitals at the end of some of the lines to form a word that fits in the gap **in the same line**. There is an example at the beginning (**0**).

Write your answers **IN CAPITAL LETTERS on the separate answer sheet**.

Example:

| 0 | D | E | S | P | E | R | A | T | E | L | Y | | | | | | | |

Two sleeps per night

Sometimes we wake up in the middle of the night and try **(0)** .... hard to   **DESPAIR**

get back to sleep, but instead we spend a really **(17)** .... night tossing and   **COMFORT**

turning until morning. This situation could be **(18)** .... of a stressful week,   **SYMPTOM**

but it could also be because of a sleep pattern we have inherited. Research

shows that our ancestors, rather than enjoying an **(19)** .... period of sleep   **INTERRUPT**

at night, had two sleeps broken up by some time awake.

The eight-hours-a-night pattern that has become almost **(20)** .... to   **ESSENCE**

modern humans has only been **(21)** .... in industrialised countries since   **CUSTOM**

the 19th century. Then **(22)** .... electricity was introduced, which resulted   **AFFORD**

in a division between night and day that became **(23)** .... blurred. What   **PROGRESS**

had until then been daytime activities could now be enjoyed after darkness,

and as a result, we went to bed later. We were therefore more tired, and this

(24) .... us to sleep through the night. However, scientists believe that,   **ABLE**

subconsciously, some people may still follow the old patterns and have a

lengthy period of wakefulness during the night.

Part 4

For questions **25–30**, complete the second sentence so that it has a similar meaning to the first sentence, using the word given. **Do not change the word given.** You must use between **three** and **six** words, including the word given. Here is an example (**0**).

Example:

0 James would only speak to the head of department alone.

ON

James .... to the head of department alone.

The gap can be filled with the words 'insisted on speaking', so you write:

Example:	0	INSISTED ON SPEAKING

Write **only** the missing words **IN CAPITAL LETTERS on the separate answer sheet**.

---

25 Do you mind if John joins us for the meeting?

TO

Do you have .... us for the meeting?

26 Dan abandoned his studies at university because he was ill.

RESULTED

Dan's .... his studies at university.

27 As soon as the tennis players went onto the court, it started raining.

HAD

No .... onto the court than it started raining.

28 'We'll have to postpone the meeting until next week, as a lot of people are on leave,' the manager said.

OFF

The manager said the meeting ………………………………….. until the following week, as a lot of people were on leave.

29 As visibility was getting worse and worse, Bob and Jane had to cut short their sailing trip.

BUT

As visibility was getting worse and worse, Bob and Jane had ………………………………….. cut short their sailing trip.

30 Please tick this box if you don't want us to inform you about future events.

RATHER

Please tick this box if you ………………………………….. sent any information about future events.

Part 5

You are going to read an article about travel. For questions **31–36**, choose the answer (**A**, **B**, **C** or **D**) which you think fits best according to the text.

Mark your answers **on the separate answer sheet**.

SEEING THE WORLD

The taxi is late, and I get nervous. Once at the airport I'm thrown into the harsh lights of Terminal B, running with my suitcase so I can wait in a long security line. My belt buckle sets off the metal detector, and my aftershave is confiscated. By now you can probably guess the punchline of this very banal story: my flight has been cancelled due to bad weather. I will be stuck here for the next 218 minutes, my only consolation a plastic cup of coffee and the predictably tasteless sandwich. Then I will miss my connecting flight and wait, in a different city, with the same menu, for another plane. It's not the flying I mind – I will always be awed by the physics that gets a fat metal bird into the sky. The rest of the journey, however, will inevitably feel like a depressing lesson in the ills of modernity, from the pre-dawn X-ray screening to the sad airport malls peddling rubbishy souvenirs.

So why do we travel? Sometimes it's because we have to, but most travel isn't non-negotiable. (In recent years only 30% of trips over 100 kilometres were made for business.) Instead we travel because we want to, because the annoyances are outweighed by the thrill of being someplace new. Because we need a vacation. Because work is stressful. Because home is boring. Because New York is New York. Travel, in other words, is a basic human desire. We're a migratory species. But here's my question: is this collective urge to travel still a worthwhile compulsion? Or is it like the taste for fatty foods: one of those instincts we should have lost a long time ago?

The good news is that pleasure is not the only advantage of travel. In fact, several new science papers suggest that travel is essential for effective thinking. Of course it's not enough simply to jump on a plane: if we want to experience the psychological benefits of travel, then we have to rethink why we do it. An Englishman, for example, might take a short break in Paris so as not to think about those troubles he's leaving behind. But here's the twist: that tourist is actually most likely to solve his stubbornest problems while sitting in a stylish Parisian café. Our thoughts are constrained by the familiar, and with a near-infinite number of things to think about, our brain spends most of its time choosing what not to notice. As a result, imagination is traded for efficiency. Putting some space between you and home, however, makes it easier to see something new in the old; the mundane is grasped from a slightly more abstract perspective. So while contemplating some delicious French pastry, we should be mulling over those domestic riddles we just can't solve.

And that isn't the only psychological perk of travel. Recently researchers at business schools in France and the USA have reported that students who had lived abroad were 20% more likely to solve a classic experiment, known as the Candle Task, than students who had never lived outside their birth country. In this task, subjects are given a candle, a cardboard box containing drawing pins, and some matches. They are told to attach the candle to a piece of corkboard on a wall so that it can burn properly and no wax drips on to the floor. Nearly 90% of people either try to pin the candle directly to the board, or melt it with the matches so that it sticks to the board. Neither strategy works. Only a slim minority of subjects come up with the solution, which involves attaching the candle to the cardboard box with wax and then pinning the box to the board. According to the researchers, the experience of another culture gives us the open-mindedness to realise that a single thing can have multiple meanings. Consider the act of leaving food on the plate: in some Oriental countries this is seen as a compliment, a signal that the host has provided enough to eat. But in many Western countries the same act is a subtle insult, an indication that the food wasn't good enough to finish. Such cultural contrasts mean that seasoned travellers are alive to ambiguity, and more willing to accept that there are different (and equally valid) ways of interpreting the world.

31 What is the writer's attitude towards flying in the first paragraph?

    A He is frustrated by the inefficiencies of air travel.

    B He is surprised by the poor standard of airport facilities.

    C He is anxious for the flight to be over as soon as possible.

    D He is resigned to the tediousness of the airport experience.

32 The writer mentions business trips to make the point that

    A relatively few people travel out of necessity.

    B relatively few journeys are taken for pleasure.

    C the majority of people travel without a valid reason to do so.

    D the majority of journeys are made for the same few reasons.

33 What does the writer recommend in the third paragraph?

    A having a holiday so as to take a rest from everyday worries

    B going as far away as possible rather than spending holidays at home

    C taking full advantage of the cultural experiences that travel can offer

    D travelling in order to gain original insights into familiar situations

34 According to the writer, recent 'Candle Task' results suggest a link between living abroad and

    A practical skills.

    B mental flexibility.

    C determination to solve problems.

    D confidence in one's own resourcefulness.

35 The writer mentions leaving food on one's plate in order to highlight

    A the difficulties travellers face when interpreting cultural conventions.

    B the importance of behaving naturally in different contexts.

    C the wide variation in levels of politeness across the world.

    D the effect of exposure to foreign influences.

36 What would be a suitable subtitle for this article?

    A How to understand the mentality of different cultures

    B How to overcome the more inconvenient aspects of travel

    C How distance and difference can boost our creative thinking

    D How other places can change the way we perceive ourselves

Part 6

You are going to read four reviews of a book entitled *Why Translation Matters*. For questions **37–40**, choose from the reviews **A–D**. The reviews may be chosen more than once.
Mark your answers **on the separate answer sheet**.

Why translation matters

Four reviewers give their opinions on translator Edith Grossman's book about her profession.

A   In *Why Translation Matters*, Grossman discusses a number of complex issues. Is a translation merely a reflection in a clouded looking glass that will never mirror the true original? Is a translator merely a sophisticated tool, a human machine soon to be replaced by a computer program? She answers these and many other questions with a lyrical eloquence that is graceful and inspiring. In the process, we are also shown detailed examples of her solutions to knotty problems; here we see her joy in discovery and doing, the best reasons for pursuing a true vocation. Such inner drive is indispensable, because as she rightly says, 'Translation is a strange craft, generally appreciated by writers, undervalued by publishers, trivialised by the academic world, and practically ignored by reviewers.' And yet, where literature exists, translation exists and it is a good thing that these issues should be explored.

B   Books by translators are few and far between. This short book was originally given as a series of three university lectures, and the ploys of a lecturer let down the writer: rhetorical questions, academic jargon. Grossman's best thinking about translation, and her best defence of translation, will be reflected in her translations themselves. It is on the rare occasions that she focuses on overcoming the challenges that her craft throws up that the book becomes more pleasurable to read. She vents her frustration on the reader, and some of this is certainly justified: translators ask for very little – simply to be read, included in the cultural debate, understood – yet almost invariably fail to be given the credit they are due. Translation, for all that it seems a technical matter, is actually anything but. It's a mode of reading so sympathetic and creative that the outcome is wholly original.

C   There is a theory that all language is a form of translation, that we speak in order to translate the unknown into the known, the non-verbal into the verbal. Edith Grossman draws upon this theory in her book, rightly suggesting, I believe, that the translation of a literary work from one language into another involves much the same creative process as that which provoked the originating author, and the end product therefore stands alone. After a rich career, she is eminently well-qualified to speak on behalf of literary translators everywhere. Nevertheless, the role of the translator is undoubtedly one of the most unappreciated and unacknowledged in the world of literature. Grossman's beautifully crafted book draws attention to this and may help to address the problem. It is accessible to the layperson and should be required reading on all university literature courses.

D   *Why Translation Matters* by Edith Grossman is based on three lectures she gave at a university in the US. As an expert in her field, she has won several awards and would seem to have every reason to feel secure, if not serene. It seems inappropriate, therefore, that she should devote entire pages to criticising publishers and reviewers, in particular, for failing to give translators the respect they deserve. However small-minded these comments may look on the page, they do form a significant part of Grossman's overall argument, which is that literature and translation are 'absolutely inseparable' and thus the translator is engaged in the very same activity as her author, and is, indeed, a writer herself. The translator's version of the text, she maintains, is to be considered an original, too. Grossman's approach is non-theoretical, as she ranges discursively over the usual concerns raised by (chiefly literary) translation in this ultimately charming little book.

Which reviewer

expresses a different opinion from reviewer A regarding how well the book is written?

37

shares reviewer B's view on whether a translation can be considered to be a new work in its own right?

38

has a different view from the others on Grossman's complaints about attitudes to translators?

39

shares reviewer A's view of the way Grossman describes how she deals with difficulties when translating books?

40

Part 7

You are going to read part of a review of a book about grass. Six paragraphs have been removed from the article. Choose from the paragraphs **A–G** the one which fits each gap (**41–46**). There is one extra paragraph which you do not need to use.

Mark your answers **on the separate answer sheet**.

The Story of Grass

John Carey reviews *The Forgiveness of Nature; The Story of Grass* by Graham Harvey

There is no doubting the radical importance of Graham Harvey's message. His case is that grass is unique among the world's plants not just in its arctic-to-equator adaptability and species diversity, but in the power of its elaborate root system to enrich soil with useful carbon compounds. The method of land management that turns this to advantage is mixed crop and cattle farming using crop rotation.

41

This traditional, nature-based farming practice received a boost in the 17th century, when it was discovered that fertility was enormously increased if the pasture incorporated clover flowers, since clover has the ability to convert nitrogen from the atmosphere into soluble soil nitrates. In the century and a half to 1850, grain yields and animal products doubled because of the clover revolution, and British farming was able to feed an extra seven million people as the industrial revolution spurred population growth.

42

When these incentives were introduced in the last quarter of the 20th century, farmers scrambled to get rid of their cattle, plough up their pastures, and turn their farms into various kinds of cereal monoculture, with fields full of single crops. These need heavy applications of chemicals to maintain yields. The high levels of artificial nitrogen that result make the crops susceptible to disease, particularly mildew, which have to be countered with yet more chemicals in the form of fungicides.

43

Intensive agriculture has had a similar effect on hay meadows. These used to flourish in Britain, and their mix of grasses supported the evolution of a rich diversity of animals and birds. Covering grassland with artificial fertiliser reverses this process. It allows one or two fast-growing varieties to eliminate the others, together with the wildlife they supported, producing monotonous acres of rye-grass.

44

In Harvey's view, British agriculture seems little more than an elaborate means of transferring money from the taxpayer to the pockets of the agrochemical industry, and laying waste the countryside in the process. The more intensive the farm, the more its owner can claim public subsidy. The European Union's common agricultural policy does not escape his attention. It has, in his opinion, outlawed the traditional mixed farm, since it requires farmers to choose between intensive crop or intensive cattle production.

45

Harvey runs the story of British agriculture alongside the story of the American prairies – flat grasslands without trees. Again the hero is grass, and the villains are well-meaning farmers with no understanding of ecology. The earliest American settlers, in the 17th century, saw no use for the prairies and labelled them desert. In fact, although arid, they were a rich and delicate ecosystem, supporting vast herds of bison which, at their peak, equalled in weight the entire current human population of north America. In three generations, all this was wiped out. The bison were slaughtered, and the prairies ploughed up for wheat and maize.

46

Now the prairies have to be dosed with artificial fertiliser and pesticides, and the government spends millions of dollars on irrigation. It is a depressing picture which mirrors the story across the Atlantic.

84

A But it's not just institutions that incur Harvey's anger, the phasing out of grass has also compounded the greenhouse effect. Grasslands take carbon from the atmosphere and lock it safely in the soil. They are far more effective at doing this than tropical rain forests, and Harvey contends that a return to grass-based husbandry would crucially alleviate global warming.

B Its presence is a result of the clearing of forest land to make way for crops and pasture. While many deplore this development it is the end result of the need to supply cheap food.

C With this system, cattle graze on fields consisting just of grass, known as pastures. After four years these are ploughed up and planted with food crops. At the same time, other fields on the same farm will now have been exhausted by food production, so they are returned to pasture again.

D The result is depressingly predictable – all these substances damage the soil and destroy its wildlife, from micro-organisms up to earthworms, insects and small mammals. The landscape falls silent.

E Farming of this kind is now virtually obsolete in the country, largely because farm subsidies encourage farmers to abandon crop rotation based on grass and to rely on chemical fertilisers instead.

F At first, yields of these crops were huge, drawing on organic matter in the topsoil accumulated over centuries. But in the next 30 years, they fell by three-quarters. Then came the 'high' winds of the 1930s, when the degraded soil literally blew away.

G This particular species spread with frightening speed in the 20th century. By 1984, the total area of species-rich grassland remaining in the country was just 3% of what it had been in 1930, and the destruction is continuing to the present day.

Part 8

You are going to read an article in which five people talk about careers in archaeology. For questions **47–56**, choose from the books (**A–E**).
Mark your answers **on the separate answer sheet**.

Which person

suggests that archaeology has a unique appeal?	47
describes how mutually supportive archaeologists tend to be?	48
criticises people who advise against studying archaeology?	49
points out the economic contribution that archaeology can make?	50
welcomes the media profile that archaeology now has?	51
points out that jobs in archaeology can often be short-term?	52
emphasises the commitment some archaeology students feel towards their subject?	53
mentions the value of an archaeological perspective on wider issues?	54
believes archaeologists often overlook job opportunities that exist for them?	55
mentions the appeal of studying a subject with a practical side to it?	56

Careers in archaeology

A Jack Stone from The Archaeological Association

The visibility of archaeology on TV and in the press has increased enormously in recent years. Whether this makes it an attractive career, given an economic climate in which young people understandably favour jobs with good salaries – not common in archaeology – is debatable, but generally, it's had a positive impact. Many archaeologists are hired by small companies to work on excavations; these jobs are often interesting but don't tend to last more than a few months at a time. Then, there are those who work for government organisations, caring for the historical environment. These jobs are more stable, but there are fewer of them. Some people stay on at university doing research and teaching, and others do museum work. In my experience, most people go into archaeology with their feet firmly on the ground.

B Dr Paul Simpson, university lecturer

It's probably what they see on film and TV, but many people assume that archaeology equals digging big holes. While this is obviously an aspect of our work, the bulk of what we do nowadays is lab-based. Few university programmes cover the ground archaeology does. Spanning sciences and humanities, it requires all sorts of skills, and in my department at least, we teach everything from human evolution to the industrial revolution. The number of people wanting to study archaeology is regrettably small – tiny relative to history, for example. Potential salaries partly explain this, but it's also down to misguided school teachers saying, 'Why not choose a safe subject like business?' Perhaps they forget it's perfectly feasible to study archaeology and then succeed in an unrelated career. Having said this, half the final-year students in my department stay in archaeology, and tend to be obsessive about it. There's something about telling stories based on evidence you've discovered – and knowing that if you hadn't discovered it, no-one would have – that cannot be experienced in any other field.

C Victoria Walker, postgraduate student

I'm researching links between Roman civilisation and Ireland 2,000 years ago, which I realise non-archaeologists might think somewhat obscure. I have a fantastic bunch of academics and students backing me up and there's a tremendous sense of being in it together. It's a challenging discipline, and one that because of the fieldwork particularly suits a hands-on person like me. Archaeology's wonderful even if you end up doing a completely different kind of job. With hindsight, I now see that the undergraduate course is as much about learning how to do things that can be used in other areas of life, like how to gather and interpret evidence, as it is about archaeology itself.

D Mark Anderson, field archaeologist

My company excavates sites before big construction projects like roads and shopping centres get started on them. Some remains date back many thousands of years, others a couple of centuries; they might be castles, temples, small houses or even just ancient farmland. Over the years, however, I've worked extensively on wetland sites like marshes and river estuaries. This means I have unusual expertise and am in demand for digs in such locations. Much of our work is practical, but we also use imagination to figure out what the tiny fragments we dig up might mean. This, I feel, is something historians, with their access to masses of evidence, tend to miss out on. People say archaeology is a luxury – today's world has far greater problems to solve than investigating how ancient people lived. It's hard to argue with this, but our troubled globe is run by people seeking quick, short-term solutions, and a deeper, longer-term understanding of humanity's history, derived from archaeology, would surely enhance their thinking.

E Tina Cray, museum manager

Even at university I was always more interested in the theoretical side of things than digging, but on graduating I assumed, like many others in my position, that excavation is what archaeology's all about. It took me a while to realise there were other paths to explore. I'm now part of a team that runs museums and heritage sites, and we provide a valuable, if underestimated, service to the community. There's the key role museums play in ensuring that knowledge of the past doesn't remain the preserve of a privileged minority. My team has also overseen an impressive rise in the number of tourists visiting museums and monuments, and this has stimulated local businesses and created jobs.

WRITING (1 hour 30 minutes)

Part 1

You **must** answer this question. Write your answer in **220–260** words in an appropriate style.

1   Your class has attended a panel discussion on how to influence people to be more environmentally friendly. You have made the notes below:

> **Ideas for influencing people to be more environmentally friendly:**
> - laws and taxes
> - education
> - media

> Some opinions expressed in the discussion:
>
> "Governments should make people pay if they damage the environment."
>
> "Schools and parents should teach children to respect the environment from a very early age."
>
> "News programmes can tell people how important these issues are."

Write an essay for your tutor discussing **two** of the ideas for influencing people in your notes. You should **explain which way would be more effective** and **provide reasons** to support your opinion.

You may, if you wish, make use of the opinions expressed in the discussion, but you should use your own words as far as possible.

Part 2

Write an answer to **one** of the questions **2–4** in this part. Write your answer in **220–260** words in an appropriate style.

---

2   You have spent two weeks at a language school in another town. While you were there, you lived in student accommodation, attended language classes, and took part in social activities organised by the school. A friend of yours has written to you asking whether you would recommend the school. Write a letter to your friend identifying which aspects of the school you were happy with, explaining which aspects were disappointing, and saying whether you would recommend the school.

Write your **letter**. You do not need to include postal addresses.

3   You work at an international company, and you and your colleagues would like to attend a language course. You decide to write a proposal to your Director suggesting that the company help with the cost of the course.

In your proposal, you should provide information about the time and costs involved and explain the relevance of the course to you and your colleagues' work.

Write your **proposal**.

4   An English language magazine is looking at television talent shows around the world. You decide to write a review of a television talent show in your country. In your review, explain what happens on the show and evaluate whether it provides positive role models for young people.

Write your **review**.

220-260.

You decide to write a
review for the 'International Students
in the UK' magazine about a concert or play
that you've seen. In your review, explain
include you liked and didn't like so much,
and how much you'd recommend this to International Students
and why.

[
[
[
[

LISTENING (approximately 40 minutes)

Part 1

You will hear three different extracts. For questions **1–6**, choose the answer (A, **B** or **C**) which fits best according to what you hear. There are two questions for each extract.

Extract One

You hear two friends talking about a geology lecture they have been to.

1   How did the man feel about the lecture?

   A surprised by its message

   B impressed by the speaker's delivery

   C interested in the visuals

2   They both think that discussions about the new geological name 'anthropocene' could

   A prove too controversial to be useful.

   B put an end to a scientific disagreement.

   C have some influence on people's behaviour.

Extract Two

You hear a man talking to a librarian about e-books.

3   The librarian says her library is considering

   A whether to provide devices for reading e-books.

   B how to stop people from keeping e-books for too long.

   C which books should be offered in electronic form.

4   The librarian is confident libraries will survive because

   A e-books are very popular with the public.

   B publishers and authors are prepared to co-operate.

   C previous technological advances haven't caused problems.

Extract Three

You hear a student, Joel, talking to his neighbour about his studies.

5   Why does the woman mention gardening?

    A to show Joel how science can be applied to everyday life

    B to encourage Joel to take an interest in the natural world

    C to advise Joel on how to keep plants healthy

6   How does Joel feel about his future career prospects?

    A Studying science won't lead him to a well-paid job.

    B He lacks the motivation to really succeed in science.

    C It is important for him to explore a wide range of options.

Part 2

You will hear an astronaut called Charles Renard talking about a simulated space mission to Mars he took part in. For questions **7–14**, complete the sentences with a word or short phrase.

MISSION TO MARS

Charles first learnt about the simulated space mission from a

[**7**] he saw.

Charles was most concerned about the lack of [**8**] inside the

simulated space capsule.

The layout of the spaceship included a dining area that was [**9**]

in shape.

The astronauts were tested on what they could remember and their

[**10**] as well as undergoing physical experiments.

Charles stresses the need to relax and practising the [**11**] was

his favourite way of doing so.

Charles explains how the crew once had to get by without water or

[**12**] for a day.

On arrival at their destination, the astronauts simulated an accidental

[**13**] to test out emergency procedures.

Charles mentions some difficulties such as a minor [**14**] that

occurred while the astronauts were eating on the return journey.

Part 3

You will hear part of an interview with two wildlife photographers called Alan Stoker and Daniela Bertram who are talking about their work. For questions **15–20**, choose the answer (**A**, **B**, **C** or **D**) which fits best according to what you hear.

---

15 Alan believes the principal concern of wildlife photographers should be

    A to secure the most impressive shots.
    B to avoid harming animals' natural habitats.
    C to develop an understanding of their subjects.
    D to keep up with the latest technical developments.

16 How did Alan feel about his assignment to photograph the birds called 'grebes'?

    A undeterred by the uncomfortable conditions
    B surprised by how well his work has since been received
    C upset that a rival photographer managed to get better shots
    D concerned that the welfare of the wildlife had been compromised

17 Alan admits that the conservation trust he has set up

    A helps to promote his business interests.
    B involves less work than collecting donations.
    C hasn't generated the anticipated level of income.
    D has changed his attitude towards his own contributions.

18 When Daniela won a major prize for her work, she was most pleased by

    A the recognition she received from other photographers.
    B the publicity given to an environmental disaster.
    C the place where the picture was exhibited.
    D the financial reward that accompanied it.

19 Daniela says she wants her photographs to

    A generate an emotional response.
    B reach as wide a public as possible.
    C bring about a change in people's behaviour.
    D show that beauty occurs in the most unlikely places.

20 Alan and Daniela agree that aspiring wildlife photographers should

    A consult with leading authorities.
    B choose a narrow field to specialise in.
    C be highly critical of their own work.
    D aim to gain a wide range of experience.

Part 4

You will hear five short extracts in which professional writers are talking about their work.

TASK ONE

For questions **21–25**, choose from the list (**A–H**) what made each speaker choose writing as a career.

TASK TWO

For questions **26–30**, choose from the list (**A–H**) what advice each speaker would give to new writers.

While you listen you must complete both tasks.

	TASK ONE			TASK TWO
A	a love of words		**A**	Ignore setbacks.
B	a desire for control		**B**	Plan a work before starting.
C	advice from a family member	Speaker 1 [ ] **21**	**C**	Read as widely as possible.	Speaker 1 [ ] **26**
D	an inspirational teacher	Speaker 2 [ ] **22**	**D**	Research the market.	Speaker 2 [ ] **27**
E	a wish to recreate the past	Speaker 3 [ ] **23**	**E**	Pay attention to criticism.	Speaker 3 [ ] **28**
F	a time of personal difficulty	Speaker 4 [ ] **24**	**F**	Write in a style that pleases you.	Speaker 4 [ ] **29**
G	a desire to escape a dull routine	Speaker 5 [ ] **25**	**G**	Maintain a healthy lifestyle.	Speaker 5 [ ] **30**
H	an interest in others		**H**	Revise your work carefully.	

SPEAKING (15 minutes)

There are two examiners. One (the interlocutor) conducts the test, providing you with the necessary materials and explaining what you have to do. The other examiner (the assessor) is introduced to you, but then takes no further part in the interaction.

Part 1 (2 minutes)

The interlocutor first asks you and your partner a few questions. The interlocutor asks candidates for some information about themselves, then widens the scope of the questions by asking about e.g. candidates' leisure activities, studies, travel and daily life. Candidates are expected to respond to the interlocutor's questions and listen to what their partner has to say.

Part 2 (a one-minute 'long turn' for each candidate, plus a 30-second response from the second candidate)

You are each given the opportunity to talk for about a minute, and to comment briefly after your partner has spoken.

The interlocutor gives you a set of pictures and asks you to talk about them for about one minute. It is important to listen carefully to the interlocutor's instructions. The interlocutor then asks your partner a question about your pictures and your partner responds briefly.

You are then given another set of pictures to look at. Your partner talks about these pictures for about one minute. This time the interlocutor asks you a question about your partner's pictures and you respond briefly.

Part 3 (4 minutes)

In this part of the test, you and your partner are asked to talk together. The interlocutor places a some text prompts on the table between you. This stimulus provides the basis for a discussion. The interlocutor explains what you have to do.

Part 4 (5 minutes)

The interlocutor asks some further questions, which leads to a more general discussion of what you have talked about in Part 3. You may comment on your partner's answers if you wish.

Frames for the Speaking Test

Test 1

Note: In the examination, there will be both an assessor and an interlocutor in the exam. The visual material for **Test 1** appears on pages C1 and C2 (Part 2) and C3 (Part 3).

Part 1   2 minutes (3 minutes for groups of three)

Interlocutor: Good morning/afternoon/evening. My name is .... and this is my colleague, ...

And your names are?

Can I have your mark sheets, please?

Thank you.

First of all we'd like to know something about you.

Select one or two questions and ask candidates in turn, as appropriate.

- Where are you from?
- What do you do here/there?
- How long have you been studying English?
- What do you enjoy most about learning English?

Select one or more questions for each candidate, as appropriate.

- Are you the kind of person who can do two things at once?
- How do you usually like to spend your free time?
- Are you planning to do any courses in the near future?
- If you could go anywhere in the world, where would you go? ..... (Why?)
- Do you use social networking sites a lot? ..... (Why? / Why not?)
- What would your ideal job be? ..... (Why?)
- Do you like to give yourself aims or targets? ..... (Why / Why not?)
- Would you enjoy preparing food for a large number of people?

Part 2   4 minutes (6 minutes for groups of three)

Unusual sports

Making a call

Interlocutor:	In this part of the test, I'm going to give each of you three pictures. I'd like you to talk about **two** of them on your own for about a minute, and also to answer a question briefly about your partner's pictures.
	(Candidate A), it's your turn first. Here are your pictures. They show **people doing different sports.**
	Indicate the pictures on page C1 to the candidates.
	I'd like you to compare **two** of the pictures, and say **why these sports have become popular, and what motivates people to take them up.**
	All right?
Candidate A:	[*1 minute*]
Interlocutor:	Thank you.
	(Candidate B), **which sport do you think requires the most skill?** ...... **(Why?)**
Candidate B:	[*Approximately 30 seconds*]
Interlocutor:	Thank you.
	Now, *(Candidate B),* here are your pictures. They show **people making calls in different places.**
	Indicate the pictures on page C2 to the candidates.
	I'd like you to compare **two** of the pictures, and say **why the people might be making calls in these places, and how difficult the calls might be to make.**
	All right?
Candidate B:	[*1 minute*]
Interlocutor:	Thank you.
	(Candidate A), **in which situation do you think the phone is most important to the person?** ...... **(Why?)**
Candidate A:	[*Approximately 30 seconds*]
Interlocutor:	Thank you.

Part 3   4 minutes (6 minutes for groups of three)

Part 4   5 minutes (8 minutes for groups of three)

World issues

Part 3

Interlocutor: Now, I'd like you to talk about something together for about two minutes *(3 minutes for groups of three)*.

Here are some issues that concern people around the world and a question for you to discuss. First you have some time to look at the task.

Indicate the text prompts on C3 to the candidates.

Now, talk to each other about **why these issues are important to people around the world today.**

Candidates: [*2 minutes (3 minutes for groups of three)*]

Interlocutor: Thank you. Now you have about a minute *(2 minutes for groups of three)* to decide **which two issues are the most urgent to address.**

Candidates: [*1 minute (2 minutes for groups of three)*]

Interlocutor: Thank you.

Part 4

Interlocutor: *Use the following questions, in order, as appropriate:*

- How important do you think it is for people to be aware of problems that affect people in other countries? ...... (Why? / Why not?)
- Some people say that it is better to solve problems in our own countries before thinking about world problems. What do you think?
- What do you think is the best way to bring world issues to people's attention? ...... (Why? / Why not?)
- Do you think that ordinary individuals can help solve big, international problems? ...... (Why? / Why not?)
- Is it important to donate money to international charities? ...... (Why? / Why not?)
- Some people believe that certain global problems are too big to solve and that it's too late to try. What do you think?

> *Select any of the following prompts, as appropriate:*
>
> - What do you think?
> - Do you agree?
> - How about you?

Thank you. That is the end of the test.

Test 2

Note: In the examination, there will be both an assessor and an interlocutor in the exam. The visual material for **Test 2** appears on pages C4 and C5 (Part 2) and C6 (Part 3).

Part 1 2 minutes (3 minutes for groups of three)

Interlocutor: Good morning/afternoon/evening. My name is .... and this is my colleague, ...

And your names are?

Can I have your mark sheets, please?

Thank you.

First of all we'd like to know something about you.

Select one or two questions and ask candidates in turn, as appropriate.

- Where are you from?
- What do you do here/there?
- How long have you been studying English?
- What do you enjoy most about learning English?

Select one or more questions for each candidate, as appropriate.

- Are you the kind of person who can do two things at once? How do you usually like to spend your free time?
- Are you planning to do any courses in the near future?
- If you could go anywhere in the world, where would you go? ..... (Why?)
- Do you use social networking sites a lot? ..... (Why? / Why not?)
- What would your ideal job be? ..... (Why?)
- Do you like to give yourself aims or targets? ..... (Why / Why not?)
- Would you enjoy preparing food for a large number of people?

Part 2   4 minutes (6 minutes for groups of three)

Thrilling moments

Discussions

Interlocutor:	In this part of the test, I'm going to give each of you three pictures. I'd like you to talk about **two** of them on your own for about a minute, and also to answer a question briefly about your partner's pictures.
	(Candidate A), it's your turn first. Here are your pictures. They show **people experiencing thrilling moments**.
	Indicate the pictures on page C4 to the candidates.
	I'd like you to compare **two** of the pictures, and say **why the people might have chosen to experience these things, and how they might be feeling**.
	All right?
Candidate A:	[*1 minute*]
Interlocutor:	Thank you.
	(Candidate B), **which experience do you think would be the most memorable? ...... (Why?)**
Candidate B:	[*Approximately 30 seconds*]
Interlocutor:	Thank you.
	Now, *(Candidate B)*, here are your pictures. They show **people discussing things in different situations**.
	Indicate the pictures on page C5 to the candidates.
	I'd like you to compare **two** of the pictures, and say **why the people might be having these discussions, and what the results of their discussions might be**.
	All right?
Candidate B:	[*1 minute*]
Interlocutor:	Thank you.
	(Candidate A), **which discussion do you think would be the most interesting? ...... (Why?)**
Candidate A:	[*Approximately 30 seconds*]
Interlocutor:	Thank you.

Part 3   4 minutes (6 minutes for groups of three)

Part 4   5 minutes (8 minutes for groups of three)

Things that annoy us

Part 3

Interlocutor:	Now, I'd like you to talk about something together for about two minutes *(3 minutes for groups of three)*.
	Here are some things that annoy a lot of people and a question for you to discuss. First you have some time to look at the task.
	Indicate the text prompts on C6 to the candidates.
	Now, talk to each other about **why these different things might annoy people.**
Candidates:	[*2 minutes (3 minutes for groups of three)*]
Interlocutor:	Thank you. Now you have about a minute *(2 minutes for groups of three)* to decide **which of these things would have the greatest effect on people's lives.**
Candidates:	[*1 minute (2 minutes for groups of three)*]
	Thank you.

Part 4

Interlocutor: *Use the following questions, in order, as appropriate:*

- Why do you think some people lose their temper more often than others?
- Do you think the pace of life today makes it more likely for people to lose their temper? ...... (Why? / Why not?)
- People say that getting angry can sometimes have a positive outcome. What's your opinion?
- Do you think 'anger management' courses can be a good idea? ...... (Why? / Why not?)
- Is it always better to show your feelings rather than hide them? ...... (Why? / Why not?)
- Do you think we become less tolerant of other people's behaviour as we get older? ...... (Why? / Why not?)

> *Select any of the following prompts, as appropriate:*
> - What do you think?
> - Do you agree?
> - How about you?

Thank you. That is the end of the test.

Test 3

Note: In the examination, there will be both an assessor and an interlocutor in the exam. The visual material for **Test 3** appears on pages C7 and C8 (Part 2) and C9 (Part 3).

Part 1   2 minutes (3 minutes for groups of three)

Interlocutor: Good morning/afternoon/evening. My name is .... and this is my colleague, ...

And your names are?

Can I have your mark sheets, please?

Thank you.

First of all we'd like to know something about you.

Select one or two questions and ask candidates in turn, as appropriate.

- Where are you from?
- What do you do here/there?
- How long have you been studying English?
- What do you enjoy most about learning English?

Select one or more questions for each candidate, as appropriate.

- Are you the kind of person who can do two things at once?
- How do you usually like to spend your free time?
- Are you planning to do any courses in the near future?
- If you could go anywhere in the world, where would you go? ..... (Why?)
- Do you use social networking sites a lot? ..... (Why? / Why not?)
- What would your ideal job be? ..... (Why?)
- Do you like to give yourself aims or targets? ..... (Why / Why not?)
- Would you enjoy preparing food for a large number of people?

Part 2   4 minutes (6 minutes for groups of three)

Being creative

Workplaces

Interlocutor:	In this part of the test, I'm going to give each of you three pictures. I'd like you to talk about **two** of them on your own for about a minute, and also to answer a question briefly about your partner's pictures.
	(Candidate A), it's your turn first. Here are your pictures. They show **people being creative in different situations.**
	Indicate the pictures on page C7 to the candidates.
	I'd like you to compare **two** of the pictures, and say **how important it is to be creative in these different situations, and how difficult this might be.**
	All right?
Candidate A:	[*1 minute*]
Interlocutor:	Thank you.
	(Candidate B), **which person do you think has to concentrate the most? ...... (Why?)**
Candidate B:	[*Approximately 30 seconds*]
Interlocutor:	Thank you.
	Now, *(Candidate B)*, here are your pictures. They show **people working in different places.**
	Indicate the pictures on page C8 to the candidates.
	I'd like you to compare **two** of the pictures, and say **why the people might enjoy working in these different places, and what difficulties they might have.**
	All right?
Candidate B:	[*1 minute*]
Interlocutor:	Thank you.
	(Candidate A), **which place do you think would be the most stressful to work in? ...... (Why?)**
Candidate A:	[*Approximately 30 seconds*]
Interlocutor:	Thank you.

Part 3   4 minutes (6 minutes for groups of three)

Part 4   5 minutes (8 minutes for groups of three)

Environmental issues

Part 3

Interlocutor:	Now, I'd like you to talk about something together for about two minutes *(3 minutes for groups of three)*.
	Here are some environmental issues that affect people's lives today and a question for you to discuss. First you have some time to look at the task.
	Indicate the text prompts on C9 to the candidates.
	Now, talk to each other about **how these different environmental issues impact on people's lives today.**
Candidates:	[*2 minutes (3 minutes for groups of three)*]
Interlocutor:	Thank you. Now you have about a minute *(2 minutes for groups of three)* to decide **which issue might be the easiest to deal with.**
Candidates:	[*1 minute (2 minutes for groups of three)*]
Interlocutor:	Thank you.

Part 4

Interlocutor: *Use the following questions, in order, as appropriate:*

- Do you feel that people are fully aware of the environmental problems we face these days? ...... (Why? / Why not?)
- Some people say that it won't be possible to reverse any environmental damage done so far. What's your view?
- Do you think it's a good idea to encourage children to cycle from an early age? ...... (Why? / Why not?)
- Do you think it would be a good idea to reward people for the amount of rubbish they recycle? ...... (Why? / Why not?)
- Charities raise a lot of money for the environment. How helpful do you think this fundraising is? ...... (Why? / Why not?)
- Some people say we should only live for today and not be concerned about the future. Do you agree? ...... (Why? / Why not?)

> *Select any of the following prompts, as appropriate:*
>
> - What do you think?
> - Do you agree?
> - How about you?

Thank you. That is the end of the test.

Test 4

Note: In the examination, there will be both an assessor and an interlocutor in the exam. The visual material for **Test 4** appears on pages C10 and C11 (Part 2) and C12 (Part 3).

Part 1   2 minutes (3 minutes for groups of three)

Interlocutor: Good morning/afternoon/evening. My name is .... and this is my colleague, ...

And your names are?

Can I have your mark sheets, please?

Thank you.

First of all we'd like to know something about you.

Select one or two questions and ask candidates in turn, as appropriate.

- Where are you from?
- What do you do here/there?
- How long have you been studying English?
- What do you enjoy most about learning English?

Select one or more questions for each candidate, as appropriate.

- Are you the kind of person who can do two things at once?
- How do you usually like to spend your free time?
- Are you planning to do any courses in the near future?
- If you could go anywhere in the world, where would you go? ..... (Why?)
- Do you use social networking sites a lot? ..... (Why? / Why not?)
- What would your ideal job be? ..... (Why?)
- Do you like to give yourself aims or targets? ..... (Why / Why not?)
- Would you enjoy preparing food for a large number of people?

Part 2   4 minutes (6 minutes for groups of three)

Being careful

Competitions

Interlocutor:	In this part of the test, I'm going to give each of you three pictures. I'd like you to talk about **two** of them on your own for about a minute, and also to answer a question briefly about your partner's pictures.
	(Candidate A), it's your turn first. Here are your pictures. They show **people being careful in different situations**.
	Indicate the pictures on page C10 to the candidates.
	I'd like you to compare **two** of the pictures, and say **how important it is to be careful in these different situations, and what might happen if they made a mistake.**
	All right?
Candidate A:	[*1 minute*]
Interlocutor:	Thank you.
	(Candidate B), in which situation do you think it is most important to be careful? ...... (Why?)
Candidate B:	[*Approximately 30 seconds*]
Interlocutor:	Thank you.
	Now, *(Candidate B)*, here are your pictures. They show **people in different competitions**.
	Indicate the pictures on page C11 to the candidates.
	I'd like you to compare **two** of the pictures, and say **why the people might have entered these competitions, and how they might be feeling.**
	All right?
Candidate B:	[*1 minute*]
Interlocutor:	Thank you.
	(Candidate A), in which situation do you think winning is most important to the people? ...... (Why?)
Candidate A:	[*Approximately 30 seconds*]
Interlocutor:	Thank you.

Part 3   4 minutes (6 minutes for groups of three)

Part 4   5 minutes (8 minutes for groups of three)

A healthy life

Part 3

Interlocutor:	Now, I'd like you to talk about something together for about two minutes *(3 minutes for groups of three)*.
	Here are some things which can all contribute to a healthy life and a question for you to discuss. First you have some time to look at the task.
	Indicate the text prompts on C12 to the candidates.
	Now, talk to each other about **how these different things can contribute to a healthy life.**
Candidates:	[*2 minutes (3 minutes for groups of three)*]
Interlocutor:	Thank you. Now you have about a minute *(2 minutes for groups of three)* to decide **which of these things can benefit people the most.**
Candidates:	[*1 minute (2 minutes for groups of three)*]
Interlocutor:	Thank you.

Part 4

Interlocutor: *Use the following questions, in order, as appropriate:*

- Some people believe we should just enjoy ourselves and not worry about our health. What do you think?
- Do you think health care should be freely available to everybody? ...... (Why?)
- At what age do you think schools should start educating children about healthy living? ...... (Why? / Why not?)
- Do you think our attitudes to healthy living change as we get older? ...... (Why? / Why not?)
- Do you think it's good for our health to take regular holidays? ...... (Why? / Why not?)
- Some people say that that laughter is sometimes the best form of medicine. How far do you agree? ...... (Why? / Why not?)

> *Select any of the following prompts, as appropriate:*
> - What do you think?
> - Do you agree?
> - How about you?

Thank you. That is the end of the test.

Marks and results

Reading and Use of English

Candidates record their answers on a separate answer sheet. One mark is given for each correct answer in Parts 1, 2 and 3 and up to two marks are given for each correct answer in Part 4. For Parts 5, 6 and 7 two marks are given for each correct answer and in Part 8 one mark is given for each correct answer. The total score is then weighted to 40 marks for the whole Reading and Use of English paper.

Writing

Examiners look at four aspects of a candidate's writing: Content, Language, Organisation and Communicative Achievement. The total is weighted to give a mark out of 40 for this paper.

Content focuses on how well the candidate has fulfilled the task; in other words if they have done what they were asked to do.

Communicative Achievement focuses on how appropriate the writing is for the situation and whether the candidate has used the appropriate register.

Organisation focuses on the way the piece of writing was put together; in other words if it is logical and ordered, and the punctuation is correct.

Language focuses on the candidate's vocabulary and grammar. This includes the range of language as well as how accurate it is.

For each of the subscales, the examiner gives a maximum of 5 marks. Examiners use the following assessment scale:

C1	Content	Communicative Achievement	Organisation	Language
5	All content is relevant to the task. Target reader is fully informed.	Uses the conventions of the communicative task with sufficient flexibility to communicate complex ideas in an effective way, holding the target reader's attention with ease, fulfilling all communicative purposes.	Text is a well-organised, coherent whole, using a variety of cohesive devices and organisational patterns with flexibility.	Uses a range of vocabulary, including less common lexis, effectively and precisely. Uses a wide range of simple and complex grammatical forms with full control, flexibility and sophistication. Errors, if present, are related to less common words and structures, or are slips.
4	*Performance shares features of Bands 3 and 5.*			
3	Minor irrelevances and/or omissions may be present. Target reader is, on the whole, informed.	Uses the conventions of the communicative task effectively to hold the target reader's attention and communicate straightforward and complex ideas, as appropriate.	Text is well organised and coherent, using a variety of cohesive devices and organisational patterns to generally good effect.	Uses a range of vocabulary, including less common lexis, appropriately. Uses a range of simple and complex grammatical forms with control and flexibility. Occasional errors may be present but do not impede communication.

2	Performance shares features of Bands 1 and 3.			
1	Irrelevances and misinterpretation of task may be present. Target reader is minimally informed.	Uses the conventions of the communicative task to hold the target reader's attention and communicate straightforward ideas.	Text is generally well organised and coherent, using a variety of linking words and cohesive devices.	Uses a range of everyday vocabulary appropriately, with occasional inappropriate use of less common lexis. Uses a range of simple and some complex grammatical forms with a good degree of control. Errors do not impede communication.
0	Content is totally irrelevant. Target reader is not informed.	Performance below Band 1.		

Length of responses

Candidates need to make sure that they write the correct number of words. Responses which are too short may not have an adequate range of language and may not provide all the information that is required. Responses which are too long may contain irrelevant content and have a negative effect on the reader.

Varieties of English

Candidates are expected to use a particular variety of English with some degree of consistency in areas such as spelling, and not for example switch from using a British spelling of a word to an American spelling of the same word.

Sample A (Test 1, Question 1 – Essay)

> Few would dispute the fact that science has a huge role in our everyday lives. If it wasn't for this intriguing and stimulating subject we wouldn't have the living conditions like we have now. Due to this fact, it is extremely important to guarantee that young people keep studying the mysteries of science. Both advertising and school programmes have been suggested as ways of encouragement.
>
> The idea that advertisements can influence young people's willingness to study science might not be wrong. Actually, if the TV gave more importance to people who dedicate their lives to the discovery of resources or other things that improve our life conditions, instead of focusing on the lives of pop stars, we would change the direction of our attention to scientists and their importance.
>
> Similarly is schools invested more on practical classes with experimental activities, the science courses would be much more appealing to all the students. However, it is also known that science isn't only fun and games. It requires a lot of hard work and students have to know the theory if they want to perform correctly the practical tasks.
>
> In conclusion, it is undoubtedly important to encourage young people to have curiosity about what's around them from an early age. and there's no more effective way to do so than to change society's ideas of what a scientist really is and how important his contributions are.

Scales	Mark	Commentary
Content	3	All content is relevant to the task, and the target reader would be on the whole be informed. Two points are discussed. However no clear opinion is given about which way would be more effective.
Communicative Achievement	5	The essay format is used effectively to hold the reader's attention and convey complex ideas which explain and justify why advertising and school programmes would encourage more young people to study science. The register is appropriately formal and consistent.
Organisation	4	The text is a well-organised and coherent whole. A variety of cohesive devices is used both within paragraphs and to link the overall text. Organisational patterns, for example the way ideas are compared and contrasted, are used to good effect.
Language	4	A range of topic specific vocabulary, including collocation and idioms is used effectively and precisely. A range of grammatical forms is used with control and flexibility. Errors are occasional and non-impeding.

[Handwritten annotations:]

conditional to present an argument. 'if ...'

The idea that.
However, in contrast
Actually ~ Go further
Give more detail..

it is undoubtedly important to...
there's no more effective way to do so than.

Sample B (Test 1, Question 3 – Report)

In this report I will evaluate the work which has been done in relation to establishing a student website. Further recommendations about the areas of the website which need developing will be given as well.

According to the requirements stated for the website, it should serve a couple primary functions, the most important of which is to inform students about local events. As it could be easily noticed the developers has met this item part of the task perfectly. There is a big section on the main page which supplies with information about anything which deserves students' attention.

Another aim which has been met is to publicise college clubs and groups. For this purpose a special pop-up window has been added to the website. This convenient tool allows students to submit their articles without registration.

And the final option which was intended to be implemented is to review products and services for students. The friendly interface of the webpages makes the website the perfect place for allocating such an information. Within one click it is possible to get an access to the detailed description of a searched item.

In conclusion I want to pay your attention to the fact that many parts of the website still need to be worked out more thoroughly. And in order to make it possible the additional fundings should be provided.

Scales	Mark	Commentary
Content	5	All content is relevant to the task and the target reader is fully informed. Details are given about the three primary aims of the website and a request for more funding is made.
Communicative Achievement	4	The conventions of report writing, for example the passive voice, are used effectively to communicate straightforward and complex ideas. The tone is objective and the facts are stated clearly using an appropriate register throughout, holding the target reader's attention.
Organisation	4	The text is a well-organised, coherent whole using a variety of cohesive devices and organisational patterns to connect ideas both within and across sentences to generally good effect. The paragraphs are well organised internally and each one focuses on a separate topic.
Language	3	A range of topic specific vocabulary, including less common lexis (*implemented; pop-up window; convenient tool*) is used appropriately. There is a range of grammatical forms used with control and flexibility. The few errors do not impede.

Sample C (Test 2, Question 1 – Essay)

International travel it's something today normal, on holidays people soften travel to other countries to show other cultures and ways of life. The business world had expanded around the world, so we have to do travels frequently.

Unless the big distances between countries, the creasingly development of the methods of transport and the media has motivated and facilitated the possibility of realise international travel.

The first and the most important factor that contributed on the international travel is the method of transport. Since we discovered the wetar, we the humans had conquered the sky.

That was a big progress to our civilization. Fly travels made easier to people to arrive to many other countries, that's because the velocity of this transport is the most quick of any other transport in the word. Also the distance travel is reduced by no obstacles in the sky which makes this transport quicker.

By the other way, the development of the media has also participated on the increase of the international travel. Today tecnology has arrived at a point that is common on our society. New tecnologies had facilitated the conexion between people and medias. This new possibility of conexion and communication between people had improved the information for everyone. So the knowledge of many other countries, the culture, places, etc. had motivated people to do travels to other countries.

Resulting, the improvement of the medias, which facilitate comunication and the methods of transport, which facilite te transport to other places reducing the time and distances, has increased the international travel.

Scales	Mark	Commentary
Content	3	All content is relevant and the target reader would be on the whole informed. Two factors have been discussed but no decision about which one has had the most impact on international travel has been made.
Communicative Achievement	2	The essay uses the conventions of the communicative task and communicates straightforward ideas, holding the reader's attention. There is an introduction and an attempt to use topic sentences to introduce ideas. The tone and register are consistent.
Organisation	1	The structure of the essay is clear, there is an introduction, a discussion and a conclusion. A variety of linking words and cohesive devices are used within the paragraphs, which are generally coherent. However, sometimes the cohesion between sentences is not always effective.
Language	1	There is a range of everyday vocabulary which is used appropriately but errors occur when less common lexis is used. There is a range of grammatical forms used with a good degree of control and generally, the errors do not impede.

Sample D (Test 2, Question 4 – Proposal)

HOW WE COULD IMPROVE OUR COLLEGE WEBSITE

Introduction
I am writing this proposal to the College Principal in order to express my suggestions about how we could possibly modify the college website to help international students.

Reaching the college buildings.
I hold the view that we should give students worldwide a better explanation on how to get to the college structures, maybe with a well detailed map, available in a wide range of foreign languages.

Information about the various course I would advise the creation in the site of a section where everyone could find an easy-to-read complete and summirising schedule that provides the students with all the necessary information about classes, timetables, teachers and books.

Social life
In a college student life a great importance is given to the relations with the others, so this aspect should not be forgotten in our modern and informative website. Creating new friendships and feeling accepted in a new and unknown country is always hard, this is why I am of the opinion that we have to dedicate a part of the site to the organization of meetings, events and other activities so as to favour interpersonal relationships.

Conclusion
To conclude, to make foreign students wish to study in our college, it is important to pay attention to the website, considering that nowadays the internet is the most powerful mean of communication through out the whole world.

Scales	Mark	Commentary
Content	5	The content is relevant to the task and the target reader is fully informed. There are some constructive points made about the website, which the Principal would be able to consider.
Communicative Achievement	4	The conventions of a proposal are used effectively to convey both straightforward and complex ideas, particularly in the use of modals to suggest and persuade. The register and tone are consistently appropriate and the target reader's attention is held throughout.
Organisation	4	The text is a well-organised, coherent whole. The aims of the proposal are clearly stated and organisational patterns are used to good effect, particularly in the use of headed sections. There is a variety of cohesive devices used.
Language	4	A range of topic specific vocabulary is used appropriately and precisely and there is a range of grammatical forms used with flexibility.

Sample E (Test 3, Question 3 – Letter)

Dear Ann,

I was very glad when I got your letter this morning. I couldn't wait to answer it. You know I am really sad I won't be able to go with you this time, but don't be scarry, going there by yourself won't be any problem. We have always gone together, but it's time you fly alone!

Believe me, I don't think you will have any kind of problems. First, airport procedures are always the same, you first check-in, then go through Police control and then you look for your departure gate, that's it! We have done this hundreds of times. I have been told that these colleges are very well-organised and that you can book a room by internet, they have a good variety of places and you can choose from self-catering single rooms to shared rooms with families within the campus. So, take your time and start sending e-mails right now. I have also heard that they have very good social programmes, so meeting new people won't have to be difficult at all, my advice is that you should contact someone in the secetary to be informed of these as soon as you get there.

Don't forget that the rest of the students will be in a same situation, and these meetings will also provide the opportunity to speak their language with foreigners and locals as well.

Although the lessons won't be difficult I advice you to take advantage of the so-called 'preparatory language courses' which will be perfect to get used to listening teachers in their natural environment before the course starts.

This will be the right thing to do, enrolle the course in any of the colleges just choose the subject and go ahead.

Kisses

Scales	Mark	Commentary
Content	5	All content is relevant to the task and the target reader is fully informed. The reader would be able to follow the advice and make appropriate choices.
Communicative Achievement	5	The letter is written in an appropriate register and functional language is used effectively to offer suitable advice and to state opinions in a persuasive, supportive tone, fulfilling the communicative purpose of the letter. Both complex and straightforward ideas are clearly communicated to the reader, whose attention would be held.
Organisation	4	The letter is a well-organised, coherent whole, which makes good use of a variety of cohesive devices to link the ideas throughout the text. More complex organisational patterns, such as the comparison between the two friends' experiences are used to generally good effect.
Language	3	Everyday vocabulary is used appropriately and there is a range of grammatical forms used with a good degree of control. Errors tend to occur when more complex phrases/lexis or structures are attempted but this does not impede communication.

Sample F (Test 3, Question 4 – Review)

Six months ago I had a pleasure to participate in an activity holiday organised by EXIS travel agency. So I'm writing in order to share my experiences and simultaneously recommend going surfing to Manly

Manly, a small town located near Sydney, isn't very popular, so you don't have to bother if the beach is too crowded. And-what's very important it's easy to get here from the airport and the journey doesn't take a lot of time. But despite all those things, it is the natural beauty of this place that amazes everyone, gold sand, tall green palm trees and perfectly pure water are really worth-seeing.

Also the hotel located in town meets all the needs of visitors. It is far from being exclusive but for sure nice and convenient. I can't also say a bad word about the staff which is always smiling and willing to help. And the food – just great! In the menu you can find delicious dishes from the local quisine. There's also a small bar on the beach which offers cold drinks and snacks. and a great option when you want to meet new people because the locals come here to listen to great live music and in the evenings to dance.

And finally – surfing. I went to this trip without any skills bit wanted to try something new. And that was a good choice. Thanks to a group of professional trainers I learned many things and also could feel totally safe. They were very patient and had a gift to share their knowledge and experience with the others. As we all know, not everyone has such ability. Also the equipment that we used was of a very high quality. On the personal note, I was glad that I could rent everything what was needed because equipment is really expensive.

Concluding, if you're looking for a good activity holiday option, you want to learn or improve your windsurfing skills, go to the EXIS office and book a trip for yourself. You won't regret any dollar.

Scales	Mark	Commentary
Content	5	All content is relevant and the target reader is fully informed. There is information about all three aspects of the holiday and a clear recommendation.
Communicative Achievement	3	The conventions of a review are used to hold the reader's attention effectively. The tone is neutral and informative, mixing fact with opinion to describe and evaluate the holiday. The ideas are clearly communicated and the reader would be able to make a decision after reading this.
Organisation	3	The conventions of a review are used to hold the reader's attention effectively. The tone is neutral and informative, mixing fact with opinion to describe and evaluate the holiday. The ideas are clearly communicated and the reader would be able to make a decision after reading this.
Language	3	There is a range of suitable vocabulary and grammatical forms used naturally with control and flexibility. The errors do not impede.

Sample G (Test 4, Question 1 – Essay)

> Our planet is a wonderful place to live on, but unfortunately we are destroying it. After a discussion among the classmates, we have reached some interesting conclusions on how we could encourage people to become more environmentally friendly.
>
> Since the situation nowadays is pretty dramatic, some argued that the government should join the cause in a practical way with specific laws and taxes because they said that the only way to open people's eyes is to talk about money. These students explained that people should pay more attention on rubbish, for example, and that politicians should do their part making pay higher taxes to those who do not differentiate their trash, contributing to the ecological disaster we are living in.
>
> On the other hand, other students claimed that new taxes are not the only way to solve the problem. They said that it is important to change people's mentality, starting from elementary school or earlier. Particular lessons on ecological matters should be introduced; teachers should talk about how every person can do her/his part in preserving the environment, such as having a shower instead of a bath, switching the light off everytime you do not need it, differentiating well rubbish, trying to avoid using the car too much, and so on. In this way, little kids would grow up knowing how to contribute to the earth's preservation in everyday life.
>
> In the end, we decided to accept both points of view since one does not exclude the other. We agreed that this is an urgent matter to take in serious consideration.

Scales	Mark	Commentary
Content	3	All content is relevant to the task and the target reader is on the whole informed. Although two ways have been discussed, there is no decision made about which would be the most effective.
Communicative Achievement	4	The essay uses the conventions of the task effectively to communicate both complex and straightforward ideas in an effective way using an appropriate register and tone. The reader's attention is held through the use of topic sentences to introduce ideas and the strong introduction and conclusion to the essay.
Organisation	3	The text is well organised and coherent and organisational patterns, such as the external references to the contrasting opinions which were offered during the initial discussion, are used to generally good effect. The text is connected by a variety of cohesive devices.
Language	3	There is a range of vocabulary which is used appropriately, including some less common lexis (*politicians should do their part; differentiate; ecological disaster*). There is a range of grammatical forms used with control and flexibility and the errors generally occur when more complex language is attempted.

Sample H (Test 4, Question 3 – Proposal)

Dear Director,

I am writing to ask the company for financial support. My colleagues and me would like to enroll in a language course to improve our skills, for we are an international company and need to speak a few languages fluently.

We have already made some research in this field and we have found a suitable course. It is 2 months long and is held in the evening hours so that we would attend it after work. The location of it is also very practical for us, as sit is only a few street away. The cost of this course is very reasonable, it is £200 per capita, so I hope the company could cover that for us. As my colleagues , some time they, often have to go abroad for business trips, I think this would be very helpful for us and also it would improve our results at work e.g. we could make deals with bigger advantage for our company. There are also benefits wining from that. having fewer but better educated workers then a lot of worse educated enables our company to love money and give bigger salaries or to refurbish the offices.

To conclude, this letter is a polite request to cover the costs of a 2 month language course for my colleagues and me. We would be very pleased if the company would do us this favor.

Yours sincerely

John Smith

Scales	Mark	Commentary
Content	5	All content is relevant to the task and the target reader is fully informed. Details of the course are given and there is a request for funding.
Communicative Achievement	2	Although this proposal is set out as a letter, some of the conventions of a proposal are used to communicate straightforward and some more complex ideas. The register and tone are appropriately formal and the details of the course and the benefits to the company are clearly stated in a factual manner, which would hold the reader's attention.
Organisation	3	The text is well organised and coherent overall. The idea of the language course is introduced and developed, and the text links how both the employees and the company would benefit, using a variety of cohesive devices and organisational patterns within sentences. However, across sentences, the linking is used to generally good effect.
Language	3	There is a range of topic specific, business vocabulary used appropriately. There is a range of grammatical forms used with control. However, there are errors with word order and linking across sentences. Although this does not impede communication, they affect the overall communicative achievement.

Listening

One mark is given for each correct answer. The total is weighted to give a mark out of 40 for the paper.

For security reasons, several versions of the Listening paper are used at each administration of the examination. Before grading, the performance of the candidates in each of the versions is compared and marks adjusted to compensate for any imbalance in levels of difficulty.

Speaking

Candidates are assessed on their own individual performance and not in relation to each other, according to the following five analytical criteria: grammatical resource, vocabulary resource, discourse management, pronunciation and interactive communication. Assessment is based on performance in the whole test and not in particular parts of the test.

Both examiners assess the candidates. The assessor applies detailed analytical scales, and the interlocutor applies a global achievement scale, which is based on the analytical scales.

Analytical scales

Grammatical resource

This refers to the accurate and appropriate use of a range of both simple and complex forms. Performance is viewed in terms of the overall effectiveness of the language used in spoken interaction.

Vocabulary resource

This refers to the candidate's ability to use a wide range of vocabulary to meet task requirements. At Advanced level, the tasks require candidates to speculate and exchange views on unfamiliar topics. Performance is viewed in terms of the overall effectiveness of the language used in spoken interaction.

Discourse management

This refers to the candidate's ability to link utterances together to form coherent speech, without undue hesitation. The utterances should be relevant to the tasks and should be arranged logically to develop the themes or arguments required by the tasks.

Pronunciation

This refers to the candidate's ability to produce intelligible utterances to fulfil the task requirements. This includes stress and intonation as well as individual sounds. Examiners put themselves in the position of the non-ESOL specialist and assess the overall impact of the pronunciation and the degree of effort required to understand the candidate.

Interactive communication

This refers to the candidate's ability to take an active part in the development of the discourse. This requires the ability to participate in the range of interactive situations in the test and to develop discussions on a range of topics by initiating and responding appropriately. This also refers to the deployment of strategies to maintain interaction at an appropriate level throughout the test so that the tasks can be fulfilled.

Global achievement

This refers to the candidate's overall effectiveness in dealing with the tasks in the four separate parts of the Advanced Speaking test. The global mark is an independent, impression mark which reflects the assessment of the candidate's performance from the interlocutor's perspective.

Marks

Marks for each of the criteria are awarded out of a five-point scale. Marks for the Speaking test are subsequently weighted to produce a final mark out of 40.

Advanced typical minimum adequate performance

The candidate develops the interaction with contributions which are mostly coherent and extended when dealing with the Advanced-level tasks. Grammar is mostly accurate and vocabulary appropriate. Utterances are understood with very little strain on the listener.

Test 1 Key

Reading and Use of English (1 hour 30 minutes)

Part 1

1 B   2 D   3 C   4 A   5 D   6 B   7 C   8 D

Part 2

9 anybody/anyone   10 like   11 make   12 for   13 by   14 have/stand
15 up   16 out/on

Part 3

17 favourable/favorable   18 unexpected   19 beginners   20 desperation
21 endanger   22 solution   23 alternatively   24 mountaineer(s)

Part 4

25 not to LET | her / the children / kids watch   26 make it ILLEGAL | to drive
27 Tom / he had left | on / in TIME OR Tom / he had been on / in TIME | leaving   28 to
be | (a) THOROUGH revision to / of / revising of   29 was a GRADUAL | rise / increase
/ improvement in   30 was of | no CONSEQUENCE OR was not / wasn't of | (any)
CONSEQUENCE

Part 5

31 D   32 B   33 C   34 B   35 A   36 C

Part 6

37 D   38 A   39 B   40 C

Part 7

41 C   42 E   43 G   44 A   45 F   46 D

Part 8

47 C   48 A   49 D   50 B   51 A   52 C   53 A   54 C   55 D   56 B

Writing (1 hour 30 minutes)

Candidate responses are marked using the assessment scale on pages 108–109.

Listening (approximately 40 minutes)

Part 1

1 B   2 C   3 A   4 B   5 C   6 B

Part 2

7 (blue) turtle   8 media studies   9 sneakers   10 oceanographers   11 shipping
12 seabird   13 birthplace/place of birth   14 icebreaker

Part 3

15 A   16 C   17 B   18 C   19 D   20 D

Part 4

21 B   22 E   23 F   24 D   25 H   26 H   27 D   28 F   29 C   30 B

Transcript	*This is the Cambridge English: Advanced, Test One.*
	I'm going to give you the instructions for this test.
	I'll introduce each part of the test and give you time to look at the questions.
	At the start of each piece you'll hear this sound:
	tone
	You'll hear each piece twice.
	Remember, while you're listening, write your answers on the question paper. You'll have five minutes at the end of the test to copy your answers onto the separate answer sheet.
	There'll now be a pause. Please ask any questions now, because you must not speak during the test.
	[pause]
PART 1	*Now open your question paper and look at Part One.*
	[pause]
	You'll hear three different extracts. For questions 1–6, choose the answer (A, B, or C) which fits best according to what you hear. There are two questions for each extract.
Extract One	*You hear two friends talking about a new office building.*
	Now look at questions one and two.
	[pause]
	tone
Man:	So, what's it like, working in that ultra-modern building?
Woman:	Well, really weird at first, but I'm getting used to it. One thing is not having your own desk, but I've worked like that before. The latest thing is that you

get moved around different parts of the building.

Man: How are people coping?

Woman: Varying degrees of success, as you can imagine. The technology available is amazing – everybody has a mobile laptop, a mobile phone, so you can work anywhere – with others, by yourself, in a funky design space, in a space like a garden. That's a bit tough – people like to define and personalise their working area – they're really taken out of their comfort zone. Work isn't a place anymore. It's what you do that counts. Teams aren't fixed either. You can be in a different one each week. But there's plenty of direction and you know what needs to be done.

Man: How do you feel about all the moving around?

Woman: It's supposed to be healthier for you – I'm not sure. It hardly matches up to a session in the gym! But sometimes you can bump into somebody unexpectedly, and it's good to bounce ideas off each other. It's thought that'll make people focus better, on their output, but that remains to be seen.

[pause]

tone

[The recording is repeated.]

[pause]

Extract Two *You hear two friends discussing business travel.*

Now look at questions three and four.

[pause]

tone

Man: So you're back from the Far East. Do you reckon the company'll be cutting back on trips like that?

Woman: Well, you'd hope they'd make more use of digital communication – things like video – but honestly, there's often no real alternative to face-to-face meetings. In certain circumstances anyway. I suppose it all comes down to being sure to book with the companies whose planes use bio-fuel. Responsible travel you could call it. Because there's no way I can foresee business travel doing anything other than growing in the future ... estimates put it between ten and fifteen per cent, or so I read recently in an analyst's report.

Man: That's certainly what they're saying – so let's hope airlines and rail companies worldwide will be responsible when it comes to planning. There'll have to be plenty of that to deal with the expected growth. All too often they just concentrate on immediate results – like the instant profit they seem to be obsessed with. Though obviously they do have to make things pay. And it's always a good thing for them if they can promote their plans by saying how much work will be provided. Above all though, what's needed is a strategy to cope with what future trends are likely to throw up.

Woman: You're right there.

[pause]

tone

[The recording is repeated.]

[pause]

Extract Three   *You hear two friends talking about some research.*

Now look at questions five and six.

[pause]

tone

Woman: I saw a fascinating programme last night – about research into human self-interest.

Man: What's to research? Selfishness is just not giving others a second thought, surely?

Woman: No – there were experiments, they showed that when you give people a financial windfall, they're happier if you insist they spend it on themselves.

Man: Who wouldn't be?

Woman: You're missing the point.

Man: So what did the research consist of exactly?

Woman: Well … they gave two groups of people a sum of cash. One group could choose between keeping it or giving it to charity; the other group had to spend it on themselves. And this second group, virtually forced to be self-interested, turned out to be the happiest. Those that voluntarily kept cash were less happy – presumably because of the undertow of guilt of having made that choice.

Man: I'm glad I didn't have to! Not easy!

Woman: One thing I took from the programme was how it's a good idea to pre-commit to any activities that are 'self-interested'. So … make plans to see friends that are hard to break, buy cinema tickets for next weekend now. You see, apparently, the less freedom you have to back out, the more fun you'll have when the time comes, because doing something for others instead won't feel like an option.

Man: Hmm … that's an interesting angle.

[pause]

tone

[The recording is repeated.]

[pause]

That's the end of Part One.

Now turn to Part Two.

[pause]

PART 2   *You will hear a man called Steven Kane giving a presentation about research into a cargo of children's bath-toys which were lost at sea.*

For questions 7–14, complete the sentences with a word or short phrase.

You now have 45 seconds to look at Part Two.

[pause]

tone

Steven: Hi. I'm Steven Kane. I want to tell you about my research into a cargo of children's bath-toys, lost at sea, which turned up in some unexpected places. About twenty years ago, an American company ordered thirty-thousand plastic bath-toys from a Chinese manufacturer, packed in sets of four: a green frog, a red beaver, a classic yellow duck and a rather uncharacteristically blue turtle; these were dispatched by sea. But en route, a storm washed the cargo overboard, and somehow the container split open, releasing the bath-toys to float away on the waves.

So how did I get involved? I'm a college lecturer but not teaching anything like economics or even geography; media studies is my field. I set my students a vacation project and one guy based his on a TV programme about these bath-toys. It made fascinating reading. Ever since, I've been trying to trace them – temporarily giving up my academic career to travel the world in the process.

Every year since the accident, bath-toys have turned up as far as Hawaii and Northern Europe, but first appeared on the coast of Alaska where I began my search. There I met people whose hobby is beachcombing. They had hoards of bath-toys to show me, along with sneakers – part of another lost cargo – as well as the regular flotsam and jetsam discarded by the currents.

But the amazing thing is, through these discoveries the bath-toys have made an incredible contribution to scientific research. For example, to obtain information about tides and circular currents, oceanographers often release a small number of drift bottles with messages inside to track where they land – but here were thirty-thousand objects to trace and document. They've provided information that's been put into use right away in the shipping industry and should eventually prove invaluable to the oil industry.

I was having great fun, but some of this diminished in Hawaii, when I was shown how the bath-toys lose their identity, in the mass of marine pollutants covering some beaches there. Rumours abounded of poisoned dolphins and porpoises and I saw the remains of a seabird with thirty-two different types of plastic in its stomach.

So I decided to investigate other aspects of the bath-toys' journey, and travelled to China in search of the factory, which I thought of as their birthplace rather than their place of manufacture. I was able to track down not only the building, but also the machine they'd been made on and the person who'd operated it.

One final challenge was to follow the route of bath-toys to Europe via the polar ice cap. An easy option would have been to board an airliner, and get an idea of the vast frozen wastes from above – but I wanted to get through though, so I opted for enlisting as a crew member on an ice-breaker – no ordinary vessel this but one tasked with cutting a sea-passage through the frozen waste. We found no frogs or beavers but I felt a renewed respect for the toys' remarkable endurance.

So before I go on … [fade]

[pause]

Now you'll hear Part Two again.

tone

[The recording is repeated.]

[pause]

That's the end of Part Two.

Now turn to Part Three.

[pause]

PART 3

You will hear part of an interview in which two scientists called Jessica Conway and Paul Flower are talking about exploration and discovery. For questions 15–20, choose the answer (A, B, C or D) which fits best according to what you hear.

You now have 70 seconds to look at Part Three.

[pause]

tone

Interviewer: Welcome to today's programme, where I'm talking to scientists Jessica Conway and Paul Flower about exploration and discovery. First of all Jessica these days surely everything on Earth has been discovered and mapped?

Jessica: Absolutely not – we've begun. You can use satellites to estimate the shape of the landscape under the oceans, for example, but it's only an estimate. In the Antarctic recently, investigating undersea volcanoes, we found a crater in the ocean floor, about four kilometres across and well over one kilometre deep and it wasn't on any map. We had no idea it was there. And that just amazed me, because there's nowhere beyond the shoreline where we can trip over such big geographical features that we don't already know about.

Interviewer: And are you finding many new animal species around these underwater craters?

Jessica: Well, as we get closer to finding everything out there, it's going to get progressively harder to find new species, but at the moment there's no sign of the rate of discovery slackening off. The real question is just how *many* more new species there might be there. At least one new species has been discovered every month over the thirty-five years we've been exploring deep-sea craters – and we've still got plenty left to record.

Interviewer: So you're clearly expecting to make similar geographical finds elsewhere?

Jessica: Sure, we're going to be exploring these sorts of features and comparing what we find for quite some while. There are still huge unexplored areas, so there'll be lots to focus our minds on in the coming decades, with the aim of all of us across different disciplines building up a kind of jigsaw puzzle of what exists where.

Interviewer: What do you think Paul?

Paul: Well … our different backgrounds make for very different research methods but the ultimate goal is the same. For example, recent work on glaciers by a US researcher has helped me re-evaluate my own data on climate change. In this business the figures can alter from day to day and you have to keep on top of it.

Interviewer: Now Paul, you've actually walked where no one's ever walked before –what's that like?

Paul: Yes – every year I go to Greenland, climb new mountains and travel on previously untouched ice caps … there are literally hundreds of these. There's a sense of freedom – I think that's what I get. You're still aware your body is exhausted, and yet by travelling to new areas every time there's this renewed feeling that this is where I'm meant to be. It's an experience like no other.

Interviewer: What about other people accessing remote areas?

Paul: You still see great areas where there are no roads, no villages, no permanent habitation whatsoever – despite the current population explosion and the need for development. I'm obviously keen to explore uncharted territory but not, of course, with the 'checklist' mentality of the wealthy globetrotter. These days of course everyone can go everywhere, it seems.

Interviewer: But surely in coming generations the urge to explore will begin to dwindle as these places are visited, catalogued, mapped?

Paul: I wouldn't want the next generation thinking, 'Huh! It's all been done before. And besides, I can get it all off the Internet.' Because you can't, you see. You can spend your life looking at a computer with the world's best search engines, but it's nowhere near the same as actually standing there on a mountain top. You can do all the research you like, but when you stand there, it's so intense, so life-giving, it doesn't matter that someone might have been there before, because now *you* are. And, regardless of your standpoint on green issues, I think people will always hold that view.

[pause]

Now you'll hear Part Three again.

tone

[The recording is repeated.]

[pause]

That's the end of Part Three.

Now turn to Part Four.

[pause]

PART 4 *Part Four consists of two tasks. You'll hear five short extracts in which people are talking about taking up a new sport. Look at Task One. For questions 21–25, choose from the list (A–H) why each speaker took up their particular sport. Now look at Task Two. For questions 26–30, choose from the list (A–H) what advice each speaker gives about taking up a sport. While you listen you must complete both tasks.*

You now have 45 seconds to look at Part Four.

[pause]

tone

Speaker One: I started judo when I was ten. I'd been good at other martial arts, so I didn't think it'd be too difficult, and I went along because my friend kept going on about how brilliant the instructor was, and how it'd do me good. I was soon taking part in competitions with people my age and older, even though I didn't think I was that great. But I got there by sheer force of will, I think, and I'd say that's the key – knowing what you think you can achieve and then making yourself go that little bit further each time. Yes, watching what you eat can go some way towards helping you succeed, but it's what goes on in your head that really counts.

[pause]

Speaker Two: I recently moved from athletics to powerlifting. It happened quite by chance – one day in the gym out of curiosity I set myself the task of finding out the maximum weight I could lift. It wasn't that much actually, but still enough to get me hooked. Although I'm still quite new to the sport, I'm keeping up pretty well, and I'm hoping to go to the USA soon to do a course with a coach that's over there who's got a great reputation. That's essential, I think – to have someone on board who knows their stuff when it comes to training. That'll take you a long way down the road to success, especially as your fitness improves.

[pause]

Speaker Three: I picked up karate a few years ago, my prime motivation being to take part in the fighting bit, I think! You're pitting yourself against another person and you've got to win. I've probably got an addictive personality where training's concerned, but with any contests I take part in, I tend to do really well as a result. It's a good feeling knowing that kids follow your example – I'd say it's a rewarding thing to fix your sights on. Obviously if you're not very good, that isn't going to happen, but if you can dish it out in this sport, your standing really goes up – and that's a good place to be.

[pause]

Speaker Four: Doing any sport brings huge rewards, and among them is the opportunity to make all kinds of friends, once you get to a certain level. And for anyone wishing to take up my sport, wheelchair racing, I'd stress the need to have total, unquestioning faith in your own ability, 'cause without that you're going absolutely nowhere. It certainly got me a long way, 'cause my international competitions have literally taken me all over the place, and I'm really grateful for what the sport has given me in that respect. And that's what I went into it for, after all.

[pause]

Speaker Five: I wasn't that keen to play badminton when my friends suggested it, but in the end it was a case of 'anything to keep them quiet'. Anyway, to my utter astonishment I turned out to be a natural at it, even beating off one or two who'd been competing for years, so that persuaded me, and I've been thrashing the shuttlecock across the net ever since. I can get very into it though, at times, and I have to be careful so that I make space for other things. My coach always tells me to maintain a sense of proportion – and I'm with him on that – after all, what's the point if it's not fun?

[pause]

Now you'll hear Part Four again.

tone

[The recording is repeated.]

[pause]

That's the end of Part Four.

There'll now be a pause of five minutes for you to copy your answers onto the separate answer sheet. Be sure to follow the numbering of all the questions. I'll remind you when there's one minute left, so that you're sure to finish in time.

[Teacher, pause the recording here for five minutes. Remind students when they have one minute left.]

That's the end of the test. Please stop now. Your supervisor will now collect all the question papers and answer sheets.

Test 2 Key

Reading and Use of English (1 hour 30 minutes)

Part 1

1 D   2 B   3 B   4 C   5 A   6 C   7 A   8 B

Part 2

9 when/where   10 At   11 being   12 which   13 in(to)   14 one
15 far   16 something

Part 3

17 innovative   18 outstanding   19 civilisations/civilizations   20 significant
21 undergone   22 enables   23 accessible   24 congratulations

Part 4

25 makes | no / little DIFFERENCE to *OR* does not / doesn't make | any / a / much
DIFFERENCE to   26 they had (got) | in MIND   27 was HELD | in such (high) regard /
esteem   28 always | COME easily / naturally to   29 to have been | MISINFORMED about
/ over / regarding / concerning / on   30 unlikely EVENT of | her party winning *OR* unlikely
EVENT (that) | her party wins

Part 5

31 B   32 A   33 C   34 D   35 B   36 A

Part 6

37 C   38 D   39 A   40 A

Part 7

41 E   42 A   43 C   44 D   45 F   46 B

Part 8

47 C   48 A   49 D   50 C   51 B   52 D   53 A   54 C   55 B   56 C

Writing (1 hour 30 minutes)

Candidate responses are marked using the assessment scale on pages 108–109.

Listening (approximately 40 minutes)

Part 1

1 C   2 C   3 B   4 C   5 C   6 A

Part 2

7 media studies   8 (a) research station   9 marketing   10 (a) travel company
11 Awesome Animals   12 shark(s)   13 back(-)stage   14 slogans / a slogan

Part 3

15 C   16 D   17 B   18 B   19 C   20 D

Part 4

21 D   22 A   23 G   24 F   25 H   26 F   27 C   28 H   29 A   30 E

Transcript	*This is the Cambridge English: Advanced, Test Two.*
	I'm going to give you the instructions for this test.
	I'll introduce each part of the test and give you time to look at the questions.
	At the start of each piece you'll hear this sound:
	tone
	You'll hear each piece twice.
	Remember, while you're listening, write your answers on the question paper. You'll have five minutes at the end of the test to copy your answers onto the separate answer sheet.
	There'll now be a pause. Please ask any questions now, because you must not speak during the test.
	[pause]
PART 1	*Now open your question paper and look at Part One.*
	[pause]
	You'll hear three different extracts. For questions 1–6, choose the answer (A, B, or C) which fits best according to what you hear. There are two questions for each extract.
Extract One	*You hear a man telling a friend about his holiday.*
	Now look at questions one and two.
	[pause]
	tone
Woman:	How was your holiday, Tom?
Man:	Absolutely fine.
Woman:	I suppose you went on one of those archaeological digs of yours? What's wrong with a walking holiday, if you don't want to lie on the beach?

Man: Nothing really – except, I'd say it doesn't give you much to think about – and that's what I really need. Lying on the beach isn't for me – I don't necessarily want to climb a mountain or do white water rafting, but a bit of exercise is good. It's nice to travel too, though to be honest, once you get down to work it doesn't matter much where you are – unless it rains all the time perhaps!

Woman: So what's the attraction of grubbing about in the ground?

Man: Finding a hoard of gold would be good, but most of us are realistic enough to know that won't ever happen. Actually I think it's good for me as a person. What we dig needs interpreting, but you'll never know for sure whether you've got it right. Others will disagree with you – and you have to respect their opinions. Some people might like to claim they're saying something really relevant that'll re-write history, but that's rather an exaggerated claim in my view.

Woman: I'm still not convinced I could do it!

[pause]

tone

[The recording is repeated.]

[pause]

Extract Two   *You hear two colleagues talking about time management.*

Now look at questions three and four.

[pause]

tone

Woman: I love watching people's expressions when they turn up late for my time management seminars.

Man: Why's that?

Woman: They sidle in looking exactly like a child who just got caught with a hand in the cookie jar, maybe mumbling something sheepishly about traffic, while their friends tease them about being late for a class on time management.

Man: But we've all done it, right?

Woman: Not me. It's causing more and more problems socially – at work, it even seriously hampers promotion chances – and I've known it sour relationships too.

Man: But what's the answer? I'm pretty hopeless myself. I've tried setting my alarm ten, even fifteen minutes fast, but …

Woman: That never works – psychologically you know it's fast – so you enjoy the lie-in!

Man: You got that right. So are you telling me you're never late? Hard to believe …

Woman: But true …

Man: So how do you do it? What's the secret?

Woman: You have to undergo a complete change of mindset – don't just aim to be on time for appointments – become an early person, period.

Man:	Hmm … sounds tough …
Woman:	But well worth it – just think: no more rushing for the train, no more missed flights, or embarrassing searches for excuses at meetings … or on dates!
Man:	Right! So how do I go about it?

[pause]

tone

[The recording is repeated.]

[pause]

Extract Three   *You hear two friends talking about a historical novel they have read.*

Now look at questions five and six.

[pause]

tone

Man:	What did you think of Lorna Dean's new book? I was disappointed in the characters.
Woman:	That's probably because you'd got so used to the ones that appear in all her other novels about the period, the old familiar friends. I thought these ones were a pretty convincing bunch – especially that rather mixed-up boy. There wasn't much she could do with the plot though – the events of the period are so well documented.
Man:	There was a lot of local colour, I thought.
Woman:	I suppose so – but it tended to be a bit over explained – the description didn't come in naturally.
Man:	Oh I don't agree with you there – I felt I got a real feel for time and place.
Woman:	This did give us a window on a very different society. The writer's view of it, of course.
Man:	Hardly fair – she'd done her research. She didn't just put her own spin on things. And didn't you think some of the politics and intrigue had a familiar ring? An interesting parallel with what goes on today?
Woman:	Oh no, I took reading it as an opportunity to forget the here and now!

[pause]

tone

[The recording is repeated.]

[pause]

That's the end of Part One.

Now turn to Part Two.

[pause]

PART 2   *You'll hear a photographer and TV cameraman called Mike Darby talking about his life and work.. For questions 7–14, complete the sentences with a word or short phrase.*

You now have 45 seconds to look at Part Two.

[pause]

tone

Mike: Hello. My name's Mike Darby and I'm here to talk about my work as a wildlife photographer and cameraman. So what does it take to make it in this profession? It helps to be a graduate, and photography degree courses are now common, although that wasn't always the case. Older photographers I work with often got into photography as a career via a different study route. One did a degree in fine art, others did media studies ... quite a few actually, whereas I graduated in Marine Biology.

I started out as a commercial diver – also ran a diving school for a while, before going on to dive in the Antarctic for a research station. It was there that I really started taking photographs underwater. At that point something clicked, I'd found my vocation, so I set up my own business as a photographer.

And I soon discovered that just being able to take a good picture isn't enough – a strong business sense is also essential, especially a flair for marketing, and sound administrative skills come in useful, as does the ability to handle your own accounts.

If you end up working freelance like me, though, it's good to keep lots of different things on the go. I've just done a shoot for a travel company. I got that tied up in four days and they kept all the pictures. A large wildlife book, however, start to finish, could take up to two years. For something like that, I'd expect to take hundreds of photos, only a few of which would end up being accepted by the publisher. But the rest don't go to waste – a magazine bought some unused ones recently. On the whole though, I sell them via a website, which sells them on to other people.

As for the books, I've actually done a number over the years. *A South African Paradise* has sold the best – it's now in its fifth reprint. But the one that gives me most personal satisfaction is *Awesome Animals*, which I did jointly with my wife. That's the real deal. And then there's *Underwater with Mike* ... I never liked the title, but it does give you a good idea of my work over the past four years.

Obviously, for me, one thrill's been broadening out into TV, doing work as a cameraman. Like, at the end of last year, I filmed stingrays in the Caribbean for a series that'll be on later this year. Before that I'd been filming all sorts of dolphins in Florida. And I've actually just finished filming various species of shark. That took me to the Mediterranean, the Indian Ocean and the Pacific.

The TV work is a bit different from the other stuff I do. It's rather more backstage because you're just a name on the credits at the end of the programme, whereas with the books you've got a whole title to your name. But within the industry it's still considered high-profile work.

Now, one thing I haven't done, but which many aspiring young photographers try, is taking film or still pictures, and then thinking up slogans, and then trying to sell both together. This can be a good way into the profession, as it gets your name known.

Now before I go onto ...

[pause]

Now you'll hear Part Two again.

tone

[The recording is repeated.]

[pause]

That's the end of Part Two.

Now turn to Part Three.

[pause]

PART 3

You will hear part of an interview in which two experts, called Kirsten Neet and Anton Best, are discussing the idea of what's called 'information overload'. For questions 15–20, choose the answer (A, B, C or D) which fits best according to what you hear.

You now have 70 seconds to look at Part Three.

[pause]

tone

Interviewer:	Hello, my guests today are Anton Best and Kirsten Neet and we're going to be talking about what's called 'information overload' – in other words, the imbalance between the information people feel they *should* absorb, and what they *can* actually absorb in practice. And though it's tempting to think of it as a modern phenomenon, I believe that may not really be the case, right Anton?
Anton:	Well, the Roman philosopher Seneca actually articulated the problem almost two millennia ago, when he complained about people buying tonnes of books and then never reading them. He felt they'd be better off mastering a few good books, and not letting themselves get sidetracked by faddish new things. His concern over a loss of quality of intellectual life was clearly expressed, and this is precisely what worries me today. I mean, even in Seneca's time there were people who were full of enthusiasm for the multitude of books – and we have exactly that kind of attitude today to overload because we have focussed on accumulating and storing and wanting more.
Interviewer:	But surely there's a difference today in terms of the sheer volume of material we can churn out at the press of a button?
Kirsten:	Absolutely, the scale of information management and accumulation we have is absolutely mind-boggling, and yet I suppose from the individual human perspective, the overload was already present with much less stuff. Of course, luckily, technology gives us the means to deal with it all with all kinds of automated methods of sifting through, so we can easily find what we're looking for.
Interviewer:	Is it possible to just do without much of this information – I mean, so much of it is worthless or irrelevant.
Anton:	We can't just shut it down and decide, okay, we're going to put our heads in the sand and ignore all this stuff. We have this material accumulated because of the labour of generations before us who often had it much harder than we did. And I'm inclined to feel that we have no option but to manage it and to teach ourselves how to use it well. I think we need to make sure we use our minds, and not lose sight of the importance of human judgement in managing information, rather than relying on the power of computers.
Kirsten:	So would you say we're getting on top of the problem of information overload?

Anton:	Well, we find that we have a whole lot of facts and statistics being thrown at us, and we find that the convenience of the Internet means that it is much, much easier to throw half a thought in an email and send it off to somebody else and sort out any queries and issues that way. But too often all that happens is a chain of incomplete messages being produced, which solves little, if anything.
Kirsten:	I think everybody, including organisations – well, they see multitasking as the general way to handle the huge increase in information, but, quite frankly, while it makes us feel efficient, evidence suggests people are making more errors and, in overall terms, taking more time. And this research is really quite at odds with the fact that people do feel as if they're being more efficient by multitasking.
Interviewer:	What are the major workplace positives for you, Kirsten?
Kirsten:	Well, quite clearly with a greater volume of information, you can do more, and if you have more readily available information, then you can respond more quickly – the fact that a business will know very quickly, thanks to social networking sites, if a customer is unhappy is a remarkable thing. But above and beyond that, I think there's an increasing involvement of the whole workforce in new lines of goods.
Interviewer:	Changing the subject completely, there must be a lot of information overload in something like the food industry.
Kirsten:	There is, yes, on dieting, for example … and there's just so much of it that if you take it all in and take it at face value, it ends up being contradictory … don't combine food types, don't eat breakfast, don't eat protein, do eat protein. So I think the message has to be to figure out what works for you and stick with it … and ditch the rest, even if that's only a minuscule part of the whole available. Maybe that attitude should be adopted towards information overload in general. Believe me, I've been through all this, and that was certainly the conclusion I came to.
Interviewer:	Let's turn now to the question of information overload in …

[pause]

Now you'll hear Part Three again.

tone

[The recording is repeated.]

[pause]

That's the end of Part Three.

Now turn to Part Four.

[pause]

PART 4   *Part Four consists of two tasks. You'll hear five short extracts in which people are talking about a course they did in business administration. Look at Task One. For questions 21–25, choose from the list (A–H) each speaker's main reason for doing the course. Now look at Task Two. For questions 26–30, choose from the list (A–H) what each speaker gained as a result of doing the course. While you listen you must complete both tasks.*

You now have 45 seconds to look at Part Four.

[pause]

tone

Speaker One: Bosses at the marketing company I was working for require all graduate trainees to do an MBA when they reach a certain level. I set out intending to return to work with more well-rounded business skills, but it actually proved a real opportunity to stop and think. I met my future business partner on the course and we had the same idea – giving businesswomen a more fashionable alternative to wearing suits. The course was a real springboard – we acquired essential skills, worked on our business plan and, crucially, built up a valuable network of contacts. We've been running our business full-time for six months now, and it's the best thing that could've happened.

[pause]

Speaker Two: I'm an international account manager and I wanted to move up the ranks in the company, so I signed up for a part-time business management course to gain a further qualification. I quickly found I could apply the things I learned to my job, and talk to my fellow students about challenges I was facing at work – and they'd help me find solutions. I soon got a job offer with an IT company as a result of my networking, and now travel the world with my job. I've more than doubled my previous salary, partly due to the skills I've learned and partly because of the people I've encountered – their advice and introductions have been a key factor in my success.

[pause]

Speaker Three: I was already working for a healthcare business when I did my MBA. On the course, I bumped into a surgeon who told me he needed a tool to help with brain-scanning. I explored the feasibility of producing it, created it and then put together a plan. A year down the line, I've graduated, the technology's just been approved by neurologists and it's all going well. So I'm really glad I did it. The fact is, I'd been thinking for some time about setting up my own company and the course seemed an ideal way to find out more about how to do this, how to work with companies, to identify markets and opportunities, for example.

[pause]

Speaker Four: I was involved with securing financial assistance for disabled people for many years, and I felt I needed a break and an opportunity to step back from it. So I decided to do the course with a view to helping people to help themselves rather than having to rely on people like me. On the course, I learned the hard skills, like finance – but also cultivated soft skills, including how to interact with people from different backgrounds – massively boosting my confidence. Getting a qualification has given me the push to work on an idea I'd cherished since my teenage years – setting up an online help forum – it's not my job but it does take up a lot of my time.

[pause]

Speaker Five: I was languishing as an out-of-work graduate when I decided to give the course a go, hoping it might open a few doors for me. I had my degree in English, but I'd never taken any business courses before. My only regret is, I wish business school had taught me more about office politics. One thing I had to learn in the real world is that you can't logically explain your way into a promotion – you have to befriend your way to success. The qualification I gained was indispensable, however, as it gave me my first real opportunity of a position in what turned out to be a great organisation – where I'm still employed today.

[pause]

Now you'll hear Part Four again.

tone

[The recording is repeated.]

[pause]

That's the end of Part Four.

There'll now be a pause of five minutes for you to copy your answers onto the separate answer sheet. Be sure to follow the numbering of all the questions. I'll remind you when there's one minute left, so that you're sure to finish in time.

[Teacher, pause the recording here for five minutes. Remind students that they have one minute left.]

That's the end of the test. Please stop now. Your supervisor will now collect all the question papers and answer sheets.

Test 3 Key

Reading and Use of English (1 hour 30 minutes)

Part 1

1 D   2 A   3 C   4 B   5 C   6 A   7 B   8 C

Part 2

9 between   10 From   11 One   12 whose   13 Rather   14 take
15 something   16 stand

Part 3

17 distinctive   18 progressively   19 dramatically   20 pursuit   21 necessary
22 ensure   23 unacceptable   24 beneficial

Part 4

25 being / living | in the public EYE   26 aside / apart FROM | the lack / absence
27 makes the album | WORTH listening   28 ONLY was the hotel | a long / some
29 was HIGH time | (that) she left   30 explain the main point | CLEARLY enough

Part 5

31 D   32 B   33 D   34 C   35 A   36 C

Part 6

37 C   38 B   39 A   40 A

Part 7

41 C   42 A   43 E   44 D   45 G   46 B

Part 8

47 B   48 A   49 C   50 B   51 D   52 A   53 B   54 D   55 C   56 C

Writing (1 hour 30 minutes)

Candidate responses are marked using the assessment scale on pages 108–109.

Listening (approximately 40 minutes)

Part 1

1 B   2 C   3 B   4 A   5 B   6 C

Part 2

7 wild dogs   8 astronomy   9 location   10 (radio) transmitters   11 (edible) plants
12 considerate   13 football   14 meal(s)/mealtime(s)

Part 3

15 B   16 D   17 C   18 D   19 A   20 D

Part 4

21 B   22 F   23 H   24 A   25 G   26 D   27 H   28 B   29 C   30 F

Transcript	*This is the Cambridge English: Advanced, Test Three.*
	I'm going to give you the instructions for this test.
	I'll introduce each part of the test and give you time to look at the questions.
	At the start of each piece you'll hear this sound:
	tone
	You'll hear each piece twice.
	Remember, while you're listening, write your answers on the question paper. You'll have five minutes at the end of the test to copy your answers onto the separate answer sheet.
	There'll now be a pause. Please ask any questions now, because you must not speak during the test.
	[pause]
PART 1	*Now open your question paper and look at Part One.*
	[pause]
	You'll hear three different extracts. For questions 1–6, choose the answer (A, B, or C) which fits best according to what you hear. There are two questions for each extract.
Extract One	*You hear two people discussing climate change.*
	Now look at questions one and two.
	[pause]
	tone
Woman:	Well, that TV debate about climate change certainly gave us plenty to think about.

Man:	Certainly did – but it wasn't what was said that worried me most. We've all heard those dire predictions before, though that doesn't mean we should take them any less seriously. Didn't it strike you that some of those speakers hadn't much of a clue? It seems understandable that practically everybody wants to express an opinion about climate change – it's going to affect us all, but an uninformed opinion doesn't have much value.
Woman:	I know what you mean. These days any celebrity, no matter what they're famous for, has an opinion worth asking, it seems. About the debate though – I think the same thing happens with articles on climate change. Obviously nobody will read them if they're too stuffy, and a bit of controversy livens them up – which is fine, I suppose, as long as journalists don't go too far.
Man:	So long as they don't think they're supposed to be jokey …
Woman:	Quite – their function is to get the message across, let the public get a true picture of what scientists are doing. But we need to know reports are accurate – so really scientists need to vet them.
Man:	I think there's always this sort of problem with research that captures the public imagination.

[pause]

tone

[The recording is repeated.]

[pause]

Extract Two *You hear two pilots taking part in a discussion programme about an aerobatics team in which they fly.*

Now look at questions three and four.

[pause]

tone

Man:	The new training session is tough, isn't it? We just eat, drink and practise flying and that's pretty hard work. But early on in the season you do improve at quite a rapid rate so I do find that very fulfilling. As you know, I'm in a new plane this year which is taking some getting used to and I've had to change some of my techniques to suit. It's been a really steep learning curve but I can't complain after making it onto the team for the world championships.
Woman:	Yeah, we stand a chance at the aerobatic championships as long as we don't compromise on the team standards. Whether we'll win or not is a different matter. The last few years we've had a good core team and since winning bronze last year our members have been steadily improving but this means there'll be added pressure on the pilots, which may go against us. We'll be lucky to get a team win but we are at least aiming for some individual medals – we've got two pilots who are in the world top ten – so that's what we're aiming for.

[pause]

tone

[The recording is repeated.]

[pause]

Extract Three   *You hear two friends talking about online book reviews.*

Now look at questions five and six.

[pause]

tone

Woman: Apparently there's an author who's been writing glowing online reviews of his own book – using a pseudonym, of course – and slating the work of other writers? Pretty shocking, don't you think?

Man: Trust you to pick up on that! There are plenty of others who are quite genuine, you know.

Woman: Well okay, maybe it is unfair to generalise. But honestly, I'd far rather read a book myself than plough through other people's opinions of one I might want to read in the future. There are reams of them, and you've no idea who posts them. People with literary pretensions, I suppose.

Man: Surely it's good to get a range of views?

Woman: I'm capable of making up my own mind, thank you.

Man: Well, I write reviews sometimes – it's not as good as swapping ideas with the other members of my reading group of course – no feedback – but it certainly does focus the mind. I'm sure I get more out of the books as a result.

Woman: So do you think it'll turn you into an author too?

Man: Don't mock! I get plenty of writing practice at work – all those dreary reports. So it's good to be able to write about something I find interesting for a change.

[pause]

tone

[The recording is repeated.]

[pause]

That's the end of Part One.

Now turn to Part Two.

[pause]

PART 2   *You'll hear a student, called Greg Pritchard, talking about his gap year trip to Africa.*

For questions 7–14, complete the sentences with a word or short phrase.

You now have 45 seconds to look at Part Two.

[pause]

tone

Greg: Hi everyone – my name's Greg Pritchard, and I'm going to tell you about an expedition I went on during my gap year.

We spent the first week camping in the Kruger National Park in South Africa – to see and learn as much as possible about the wildlife there.

There's an amazing range of animals – some of the biggest like elephants, lions and rhinos, as well as more wild dogs than in any other part of South Africa. Can you believe there are also five hundred and seventeen species of birds and a hundred and fourteen different kinds of reptiles?

During the study sessions, we could choose from quite a range of subjects. Climatology was popular – not surprising because of climate change – and animal behaviour was an obvious favourite. I opted for astronomy and hadn't expected to be part of such a large group.

Week Two was the conservation project – we left the park for the Olifants Gorge, the largest breeding ground for the Nile crocodile. Large numbers of crocodiles are dying – it's important to find out why. A huge dam has been built and it seems the real cause of the trouble is that the river isn't free-flowing anymore.

We helped with a survey to find how many crocodiles live around the dam. I took part in night patrols – in a boat. My partner had to estimate the length of each crocodile we saw, and I noted its location on a hand held GPS. We were told that once this part of the survey was complete there are plans to plot crocodile movements. Twelve fully-grown crocodiles will have radio transmitters fitted to their necks and younger crocodiles – easier to catch and deal with – will have colour-coded tags fixed on their tails.

It was quite a big change to spend the third week on a wilderness trail in the bush. We had no timetable – just walked by day and camped wherever we got to at night. I knew we wouldn't starve – we had just enough provisions to last – but we were encouraged to fend for ourselves. It wasn't too difficult to catch fish, but I was pretty chuffed that I identified some edible plants which we could cook for supper one night. We learnt a lot of practical things, like how to find water and build a shelter – and how to get on with each other. I think I got to be more considerate, though I'm sure the idea is to make people more self-reliant.

We spent the final week in a village on the coast. I'd been a bit alarmed about this actually, because helping in the local school was mentioned and I wasn't sure I'd manage with teaching anything like maths – but fortunately football seems universal and my coaching in that went down well.

During that last week we experienced a different way of life – completely different from our own. I enjoyed going out on trips with the local fishermen, and joining a family for meals turned out to be the best way to find out about them and their customs. There were plenty of other things to enjoy there – kayaking sessions on the lagoon and snorkelling on the reef. It was a truly wonderful, and varied, four weeks.

[pause]

Now you'll hear Part Two again.

tone

[The recording is repeated.]

[pause]

That's the end of Part Two.

Now turn to Part Three.

[pause]

PART 3   *You'll hear part of an interview with two board game enthusiasts called Sarah Walters and Ed Zander about the renewed popularity of traditional board games. For questions 15–20, choose the answer (A, B, C or D) which fits best according to what you hear.*

You now have 70 seconds to look at Part Three.

[pause]

tone

Interviewer:	Hello and welcome to the programme, where this week we are discussing, traditional, non-digital board games, such as Monopoly and Scrabble. With me are two enthusiasts, Sarah Walters and Ed Zander. Sarah, why do you think traditional board games are becoming more popular again?
Sarah:	Well, they were originally designed for families. Consequently the themes are not typically your fantasy-type aliens or dragons, they're much more from everyday life – anything from farming to creating your own home. Additionally, we're in a culture where, thanks to recent rapid changes, it's very rare now to meet people who don't play digital games and as a result we are far more accepting of play for adults as a legitimate pastime. But the thing is that most games are played on screens. In a world where everything appears to be mediated through an electronic device of some kind, there's a growing desire to put games back on the living room table.
Interviewer:	And Ed, what do you think this century holds for game-playing?
Ed:	Well, people say that our lives are more pressurised and games are a welcome outlet for this, but I would argue there's much more to it than that. Yes, this century is going to be one of play but the way we work and learn, communicate with each other, socialise and form new relationships – all these essential aspects of our lives are increasingly carried out via the Internet and digital networks. And games, be they digital or traditional, will always mirror these things.
Interviewer:	But what, specifically, is their attraction?
Sarah:	Digital technology can be isolating, despite social networks and emailing. There's a growing nostalgia for real interaction. At the same time people are looking for leisure activities that involve solving problems, rather than just passively watching television stories. Board games let us play directly with each other, intimately, face-to-face. And maybe part of our brain really likes being in a room with other people. The most fun I have playing games, it's not with computers, it's playing board games with friends.
Interviewer:	Is this phenomenon the same the world over?

Ed:	Well in parts of Europe board games are integral to the culture – people seem to live and breathe board games the way we do videogames in the USA. For example, they release over six hundred brand-new board games at Germany's Essen Convention every single year. So there's just a massive amount. And participants are all very excited, they've read up extensively on what the latest hot game is. So as soon as the doors open they can make a beeline for the stalls and get their special game, and just sit down and start playing it. So it's just crazy, enthusiastic board gaming – I've never seen anything like it, it's just amazing.
Interviewer:	And … isn't there some kind of award for the best game each year?
Sarah:	Absolutely, the game of the year award, which was started in 1979 in Germany, it's become a real stamp of quality. In the USA when somebody goes looking for a board game, they might think about trying something new but they'll usually end up leaving with something they've played before and played as a child. But in Germany if you see that little red shape on the box, that seal of approval given to games shortlisted for the award, you know it's going to be a good one. So you get people trying new games all the time. And the press have picked up on this too – the event gets great coverage every year.
Interviewer:	So tell us about your own collections?
Sarah:	Yes, I've got a huge collection – it's hard to resist that temptation to hang on to them … they're all so well-crafted. But you know there are game players and then there are 'collectors', but I'm afraid I'm both! I've actually converted my basement into a games room, and yes, I've got a lot – I never discard any on principle. Might be worth something one day, you see.
Ed:	I tried to get rid of some … you know, if I wasn't playing them I'd try to chuck a few out, but then a couple of times that rebounded on me, and I've really wished I hadn't got rid of them. So I've stopped doing that. Now, if I buy one, I'm just going to keep it.
Interviewer:	So let me move onto recent developments. Have there been any …

[pause]

Now you'll hear Part Three again.

tone

[The recording is repeated.]

[pause]

That's the end of Part Three.

Now turn to Part Four.

[pause]

PART 4

Part Four consists of two tasks. You'll hear five short extracts in which people are talking about having more than one job at a time. Look at Task One. For questions 21–25, choose from the list (A–H) why each speaker took on more than one job. Now look at Task Two. For questions 26–30, choose from the list (A–H) the unexpected result of having more than one job that each speaker refers to. While you listen you must complete both tasks.

You now have 45 seconds to look at Part Four.

[pause]

tone

Speaker One: I'm currently holding down three roles – sales executive, market stall holder and online jewellery entrepreneur. It's quite a challenge but not being on a standard career path isn't a worry – that's for traditionalists. I'm not interested in tying myself down to a single job somewhere. Today's workforce is much more fluid, and as long as you're proactive, you can make your own path. The best opportunities come from meeting people – the greater variety of people you come across, the better. Having three jobs has certainly led to a huge increase in my circle of acquaintances across the country – including my husband-to-be, who was a regular customer at my stall!

[pause]

Speaker Two: Weekdays I'm in recruitment, but I spend Friday nights at home baking bread to sell at the local Saturday market. I originally did it partly to earn some extra money, but more because I wanted to do something for me – you know … make something completely from scratch. I never dreamed it would take off the way it has. Now it's more about how I can improve the process – the money is still just a bonus. I think this phenomenon of working in multiple roles has taken hold because my generation wants more from work than just a way to pay the rent. I know I wanted a feeling of fulfilment – and I expect my work to reflect my values.

[pause]

Speaker Three: I still work as a school drama teacher on a part-time basis but I stopped my full-time post there so that I could do what I'd always wanted to do, which was to be a freelance theatre director. In many ways the directing is merely a continuation of what I was doing before with plays and musicals at school. The flexibility of the lifestyle is a huge bonus – I was lucky enough to be able to work with an award-winning director recently in a local theatre project, a chance that came completely out of the blue. I could never have done it with a traditional '40-hour week' job. What I do doesn't feel like work, it's creative and enterprising.

[pause]

Speaker Four: Being an electrician and a model may seem weird, but then as an ex-army man living on a houseboat, I don't really fit into the usual categories. An electrician's job alone would never have done me after life in the military – it was the variety I still craved. So being asked to do a magazine cover, even a lesser-known one, after only three months modelling was simply a stunning bonus. I love being a freelancer with more than one career – it means a whole new work ethic because it makes you care more. In a salaried job you can just sit around and you'll always get paid, whereas in my line you're only as good as your last day's work.

[pause]

Speaker Five: I was once a full-time DJ at a nightclub, which I loved, but I got really fed up with dealing with unreasonable customers. I wanted a new departure. Sure, I still play now, but only on occasional club nights and at wedding receptions, earning enough to cover the rent on my studio, where I specialise in designing clothes. So my two jobs couldn't be more diverse. I put in as many hours as I possibly can, and do the best that I can do. It's all I really care about – work comes first and nothing else is important. Winning a prestigious design award though – I didn't see that coming! I haven't had a holiday for three years, but I don't mind one little bit!

[pause]

Now you'll hear Part Four again.

tone

[The recording is repeated.]

[pause]

That's the end of Part Four.

There'll now be a pause of five minutes for you to copy your answers onto the separate answer sheet. Be sure to follow the numbering of all the questions. I'll remind you when there's one minute left, so that you're sure to finish in time.

[Teacher, pause the recording here for five minutes. Remind students that they have one minute left.]

That's the end of the test. Please stop now. Your supervisor will now collect all the question papers and answer sheets.

Test 4 Key

Reading and Use of English (1 hour 30 minutes)

Part 1

1 D   2 C   3 A   4 A   5 B   6 B   7 A   8 D

Part 2

9 Having   10 myself   11 except/but   12 if/when(ever)   13 made   14 no/without
15 even   16 what

Part 3

17 uncomfortable   18 symptomatic   19 uninterrupted   20 essential   21 customary
22 affordable   23 progressively   24 enabled

Part 4

25 any objection(s) / an objection TO | John('s) joining   26 illness / sickness RESULTED in |
him / his abandoning / the abandonment of   27 sooner HAD | the tennis players gone /
got / come   28 would have / need to be | put / called OFF OR had to be | put / called OFF
29 no (other) choice / alternative / option | BUT to   30 'd / would RATHER | not be

Part 5

31 D   32 A   33 D   34 B   35 D   36 C

Part 6

37 B   38 C   39 D   40 B

Part 7

41 C   42 E   43 D   44 G   45 A   46 F

Part 8

47 B   48 C   49 B   50 E   51 A   52 A   53 B   54 D   55 E   56 C

Writing (1 hour 30 minutes)

Candidate responses are marked using the assessment scale on pages 108–109.

Listening (approximately 40 minutes)

Part 1

1 A   2 C   3 A   4 C   5 A   6 C

Part 2

7 website (ad/advertisement)   8 (the) sun   9 oval   10 mental reactions   11 guitar
12 communication links   13 fall   14 argument

Part 3

15 C   16 A   17 D   18 B   19 A   20 B

Part 4

21 F   22 G   23 D   24 B   25 H   26 E   27 C   28 G   29 H   30 B

Transcript	*This is the Cambridge English: Advanced, Test Four.*
	I'm going to give you the instructions for this test.
	I'll introduce each part of the test and give you time to look at the questions.
	At the start of each piece you'll hear this sound:
	tone
	You'll hear each piece twice.
	Remember, while you're listening, write your answers on the question paper. You'll have five minutes at the end of the test to copy your answers onto the separate answer sheet.
	There'll now be a pause. Please ask any questions now, because you must not speak during the test.
	[pause]
PART 1	*Now open your question paper and look at Part One.*
	[pause]
	You'll hear three different extracts. For questions 1–6, choose the answer (A, B, or C) which fits best according to what you hear. There are two questions for each extract.
Extract One	*You hear two friends talking about a geology lecture they have been to.*
	Now look at questions one and two.
	[pause]
	tone
Man:	So according to the lecture, we're living in what some geologists and scientists want to call the 'Anthropocene age', the Age of Man.

Woman:	It was certainly an eye-opener for me.
Man:	Me too … all that human activity … mining, damming rivers, deforestation, agriculture and the use of chemicals. I didn't realise it's made as much impression on the planet as major catastrophes – like eruptions and meteor strikes. Pretty much doom and gloom, I suppose, and the speaker lectured in a style to match, didn't he?
Woman:	Yes – not an inspiring guy.
Man:	I'd seen all those charts and diagrams he used before in college. But anyway, what do you think about the actual name ... you know, anthropocene?
Woman:	It's OK – if you know what it means. I think the good thing would be if labelling this period made people change their ways. But he did say that scientists are arguing about whether it's a valid concept. Do you think they'll ever agree with each other?
Man:	Maybe – though sometimes debates like this can get pretty nasty, I believe. But that's not the point – we need to re-assess the way we do things.
Woman:	And they'll have to change all those charts of geological time scales!

[pause]

tone

[The recording is repeated.]

[pause]

Extract Two   *You'll hear a man talking to a librarian about e-books.*

Now look at questions three and four.

[pause]

tone

Man:	What is the e-book – in the library's definition? I can't find one on the shelf, can I?
Woman:	Good question – the narrow definition is a digital copy of a physical book that you download to a reading device.
Man:	So suppose there's a book I want to read and I think it's available on e-books and I want to read it. What happens?
Woman:	Not every title you're interested in reading is available through your library – there's a selection process naturally. You get on the library website – and download the book if it's there.
Man:	So I borrow the book and read it – on my iPad or whatever.
Woman:	Many libraries loan out e-readers – we're still mulling it over though.
Man:	And late fees – if I hang on to it too long?
Woman:	That's organised – the e-book simply disappears from your device. I think that's a nice thing about it.

Man:	But in a way aren't you kind of spelling the end of libraries?
Woman:	Well, libraries have transitioned successfully over a variety of formats in the past – think about CDs and music downloads. That's proof enough for me that libraries have a future. Besides, at the moment e-books are very much in demand and we've got good partnerships with publishers and authors.
Man:	Thanks – that puts things into perspective.

[pause]

tone

[The recording is repeated.]

[pause]

Extract Three   *You hear a student, Joel, talking to his neighbour about his studies.*

Now look at questions five and six.

[pause]

tone

Woman:	Hey Joel, how's college going?
Man:	Oh hi Mrs Stone – Well, I do like the fact I'm majoring in science, but I'm struggling to get to grips with it at times.
Woman:	Well I know it can seem very abstract and theoretical at times, but after sitting in front of a computer screen all day at work, I love to get outside in the garden. It's such a nice change of pace.
Man:	I'm not sure I follow.
Woman:	Well, back in March we bought these plants but soon after they turned sickly because the soil was too alkaline, so we put down sulphur to slowly turn the soil more acidic.
Man:	Well they look healthy now!
Woman:	Exactly, but behind it all was chemistry. You might not like gardening but it shows science's importance.
Man:	I guess my main question is how relevant my studies are to my future.
Woman:	I wouldn't worry. Is it purely science you want to do? I've heard scientific jobs aren't as well paid as they used to be.
Man:	Oh I'm sure working for some multi-national company would pay well but I'm not sure if that's the way I want to go. There are lots of related careers which might be more rewarding, intellectually as well as financially I mean. Money's nice but it's not the thing which really inspires me.

[pause]

tone

[The recording is repeated.]

[pause]

That's the end of Part One.

Now turn to Part Two.

[pause]

PART 2   *You will hear an astronaut called Charles Renard talking about a simulated space mission to Mars he took part in. For questions 7–14, complete the sentences with a word or short phrase.*

You now have 45 seconds to look at Part Two.

[pause]

tone

Charles: I've recently returned from Mars! Well, actually, that's not quite true – the spaceship I was in … with its five-man crew never left the ground. It was in fact a simulated space mission for research purposes.

The idea of becoming an astronaut has always appealed to me. I loved science-fiction stories as a kid, studied physics at college, and I still enjoy magazine articles on any aspects of space. I've always browsed any relevant website on the off-chance of finding work. When I saw this project advertised I jumped at the chance, and was thrilled to be accepted.

To simulate life in a spaceship, I'd be living in a windowless area no larger than a bus, with five strangers – and some aspects of sealing myself off from the world for so long did worry me, naturally. Like I wouldn't be able to step outside, breathe fresh air or, crucially, feel the sun on my face, and nobody knew how the whole experiment would affect the crew psychologically.

Yet I felt a tremendous sense of excitement when I entered the spaceship itself. Inside, it was surprisingly pleasant, with six square cabins, and an oval section where we would have our meals. There was also a medical module – a long cylinder that doubled as the laboratory and a utility module that contained a gym.

A typical day began at eight a.m. with medical checks, followed by experiments, including those focused on cognitive tasks – covering things like memory and mental reactions, in addition to physical tests involving the wearing of electrodes to see if our bodies were changing during the mission.

Obviously there were times when we needed to relax. Every so often we'd take breaks for training in the gym, especially on the rowing machine, and in the evening I'd try my Russian on a colleague or play my guitar, which I found the most effective way to unwind. We all got along well – at times it felt like being back at college.

Every so often, the team behind the scenes would stage an emergency to see how we'd cope – like when our communication links and supplies of water were cut off for twenty-four hours once after an imaginary fire. And though the support crew were, in reality, only twenty metres away, it was hard to shake the sense they were millions of kilometres distant.

A month later we'd 'reached' the red planet. On a mocked-up landscape, space-suited crew members collected soil and rock samples and drove computer-simulated vehicles, even performing a deliberate fall, to test how easy it'd be to recover from an accident.

   In contrast, the return journey was punishingly monotonous. My crewmates became more important than ever then – but problems could arise. I like to discuss things at mealtimes, for example, but one of the other guys didn't and on one occasion it led to an argument. We made up quickly though – that's important in such a confined environment.

   Finally it was all over. We'd travelled seventy million miles without moving a centimetre, and somehow remained friends through it all.

[pause]

Now you'll hear Part Two again.

tone

[The recording is repeated.]

[pause]

That's the end of Part Two.

Now turn to Part Three.

[pause]

PART 3   *You will hear part of an interview with two wildlife photographers called Alan Stoker and Daniela Bertram, who are talking about their work. For questions 15–20, choose the answer (A, B, C or D) which fits best according to what you hear.*

You now have 70 seconds to look at Part Three.

[pause]

tone

Interviewer: With me today are the acclaimed wildlife photographer, Alan Stoker, and Daniela Bertram, who's just won a major prize for wildlife photography. Alan – you're reportedly concerned about declining professional ethics in wildlife photography. What do you mean by that?

Alan: I meant simply that for many photographers nowadays, capturing a striking image seems to have taken precedence over the satisfaction to be gained from the actual process of securing it. For me, wildlife photography's all about getting close to something that's alive; gaining an insight into the reality of its daily life. That brings a responsibility to the creatures you photograph that transcends any technical considerations about equipment, processing software or whatever. And if this attitude sometimes affects the saleability of my pictures, then so be it. I have no problem with that. Financing the activity should be the means to an end – not vice versa.

Interviewer: So how do you tackle an assignment?

Alan: Well, I worked on a project to photograph birds called 'grebes' this summer. They nest around inland waterways and to get the shots I wanted, without disturbing them, I had to crouch in freezing cold water under a dense thorn bush – I was scratched to pieces and chilled to the bone, but wouldn't have missed it for the world. The project was deemed a success – all the young birds fledged safely and we've had modest sales for the images. My pictures will never set the world alight – some of the other photographers involved got much better ones and I don't begrudge them that – I still see every shoot as part of a long learning process really – so I'm not prone to disappointment!

Interviewer: And you've also set up a wildlife conservation trust, I believe?

Alan: That's right. I feel a real need both to contribute myself to conservation initiatives, and to encourage others to do so. But, asking people for money's always difficult. I've generally made my own contributions behind the scenes in the past – I'm not into grand gestures or anything, but I'm beginning to see the virtue of leading by example. What we've done is set up a scheme whereby anyone buying one of my endorsed photosets also makes a fixed-percentage payment to the trust. It's wholly transparent, yet cynics claim it's just a way of marketing the products. But I promise you the hassle involved in setting these things up would hardly make that a cost-effective proposition.

Interviewer: I think Daniela should come in here – after all, her prize winning photograph was of birds having their feathers cleaned after an oil spill. How do you feel about your win?

Daniela: It was a dream come true! It would be quite ridiculous to claim I wasn't pleased about the prize money, but what was happening in the area affected by the spill was far more significant than anything else – and my photo shone a light on that and that was uniquely gratifying. Even some of the other photographers whose work was up for the award have been amazingly supportive of the cause – and the Natural History Museum – did you know the picture's exhibited there? – Well that's been one of my favourite places since I was a child, so that was brilliant too.

Interviewer: So your approach to wildlife photography and conservation issues is quite different from Alan's?

Daniela: Well first of all, let me say how much I admire Alan's work, but my background is as a photojournalist – so for me pictures tell stories. The oil spill for instance was awful, but strangely there was some beauty to be found in it. I'm interested in people thinking about what they're looking at and being moved by it. There's seven billion of us on the planet, and if we want to be here for the long haul, we need to start looking after it. I don't know about creating change in attitudes – how on earth to quantify that? – But waking people up to the situation's perfectly possible.

Interviewer: Finally, both of you, what about some advice for people just entering wildlife photography?

Alan: My tip for anyone starting up is to indulge their passion, shoot away, but go for depth. My work focuses on a narrow range of species – but where I win is what my pictures tell you about those species. What do you think, Daniela?

Daniela: Well I don't consider myself a wildlife photographer, I'm a conservation photographer, so I guess I'm pretty single-minded too. But I'd also say, be a ruthless editor – don't show substandard work because you'll live to regret it.

Alan: And I learn about animals and where to find them from experts in the field – reserve managers, gamekeepers, researchers – I've referred to them all.

Daniela:	Sure – and that's right for your kind of work, less so for mine. I'd have no problems going along with depth rather than breadth though – shoot away by all means, indulge your passion but don't kid yourself your stuff's any better than it really is.
Interviewer:	There we must stop. Thank you both ...

[pause]

Now you'll hear Part Three again.

tone

[The recording is repeated.]

[pause]

That's the end of Part Three.

Now turn to Part Four.

[pause]

PART 4	*Part Four consists of two tasks. You'll hear five short extracts in which professional writers are talking about their work. Look at Task One. For questions 21–25, choose from the list (A–H) what made each speaker choose writing as a career. Now look at Task Two. For questions 26–30, choose from the list (A–H) what advice each speaker would give to new writers. While you listen you must complete both tasks.*
	You now have 45 seconds to look at Part Four.

[pause]

tone

Speaker 1:	I first put pen to paper in a serious way when I was sixteen and undergoing what seemed then a huge rollercoaster ride of a time. Anyway, in order to cope I jotted it all down in amazing detail. I must have been unbearable because Mum kept telling me to take up a new interest, though she meant something more sociable I think. Anyway, I've stuck at it and learned a few things along the way, like not ignoring any feedback – be it positive or negative. Most of it is rubbish but there can be a few gold nuggets too. People tell you to rise above rejections from publishers and so on, but that's easier said than done in my experience.

[pause]

Speaker 2:	When would-be writers ask for tips, I think they're hoping I'll give them the secret to getting published, something like 'find out what the average reader's buying, then imitate it and the world of books will open to you'. Would that it were that easy! It seems odd to say 'become a consumer of the written word in all its forms and that'll inform your own work', but that's it really. You see, as a teenager I felt too intimidated in class to express my adolescent feelings. It was only when I ended up in a dreary office drafting reports on tedious products that I started writing lively pieces for magazines to break out of the daily grind.

[pause]

Speaker 3:   I started writing thanks to some really stimulating classes given by someone who made the written word come alive. It was this which helped me subsequently develop a fascination with what language can do. My agent is keen on the notion that the learning process never ends – so, although it's tempting to tear up rejection letters, it's best to resist the urge and refer back to them every time you write a new piece of work. What I'd pass on is to make sure you don't neglect your general well-being as your overall stamina helps the writing process, which demands strength of all sorts.

[pause]

Speaker 4:   I'd always recommend being professional, rather than writing purely to gratify yourself. To my mind, clarity is key. It's so tempting to submit the first draft of a novel you've struggled over for years once you've typed the last page. If it's shelved for a while, and then worked through dispassionately, the end result will be much sharper. As to how it began, well, at high school I yearned to be an actor, but I was far too shy. Writing plays felt safer, and meant I could be in charge of my own little world. I think our drama teacher had a hand in it too although unintentionally. She was rather overwhelming, so retreat seemed the only course of action!

[pause]

Speaker 5:   In primary school, I wrote stories in my head while the teacher was doing her best to explain poetry to us. The thing that was really instrumental in getting me going though, were my parents' parties. I'd try to look bored, but all the time I was intrigued by the guests, soaking up half-understood snippets of conversation to jot down later. One thing I'd like to suggest, when setting out on a novel it's crucial to have an outcome in mind. Of course this may change along the way, but without one you'll just meander along and lose impetus. That's why reading other people's work can be counterproductive. You could just end up unintentionally with a carbon copy of something.

[pause]

Now you'll hear Part Four again.

tone

[The recording is repeated.]

[pause]

That's the end of Part Four.

There'll now be a pause of five minutes for you to copy your answers onto the separate answer sheet. Be sure to follow the numbering of all the questions. I'll remind you when there's one minute left, so that you're sure to finish in time.

[Teacher, pause the recording here for five minutes. Remind students when they have one minute left.]

That's the end of the test. Please stop now. Your supervisor will now collect all the question papers and answer sheets.

CAMBRIDGE ENGLISH
Language Assessment
Part of the University of Cambridge

Do not write in this box

SAMPLE

Candidate Name
If not already printed, write name
in CAPITALS and complete the
Candidate No. grid (in pencil).

Candidate Signature

Examination Title

Centre

Supervisor:
If the candidate is ABSENT or has WITHDRAWN shade here

Centre No.

Candidate No.

Examination
Details

Candidate Answer Sheet 1

Instructions

Use a PENCIL (B or HB). Rub out any answer you wish to change using an eraser.

Part 1: Mark ONE letter for each question.

For example, if you think **B** is the right
answer to the question, mark your
answer sheet like this:

Parts 2, 3 and **4:** Write your answer clearly
in CAPITAL LETTERS.

For Parts 2 and 3 write one letter
in each box. For example:

Part 1				
1	A	B	C	D
2	A	B	C	D
3	A	B	C	D
4	A	B	C	D
5	A	B	C	D
6	A	B	C	D
7	A	B	C	D
8	A	B	C	D

Part 2

Do not write below here

9
10
11
12
13
14
15
16

Continues over ➡

CAE CPE R1

DP801

© UCLES 2014   Photocopiable

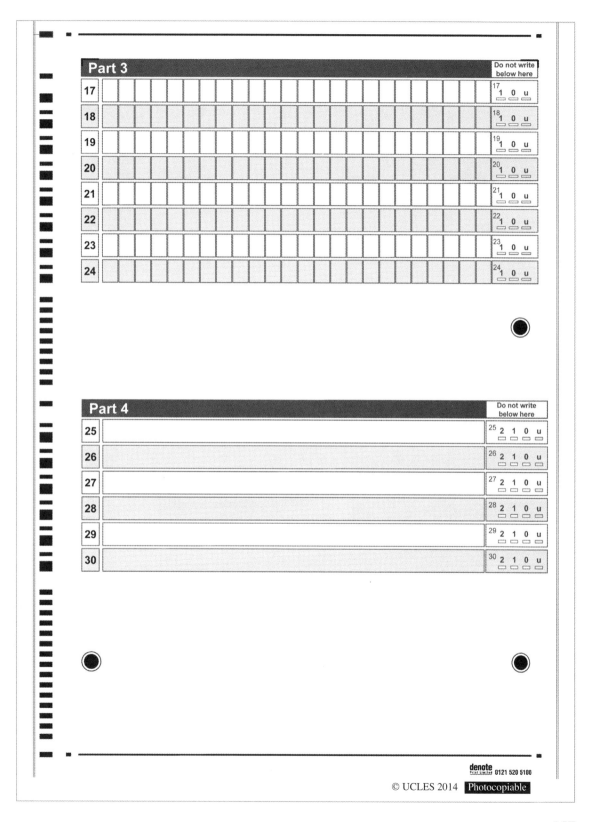

Part 3

		Do not write below here
17		17 1 0 u
18		18 1 0 u
19		19 1 0 u
20		20 1 0 u
21		21 1 0 u
22		22 1 0 u
23		23 1 0 u
24		24 1 0 u

Part 4

		Do not write below here
25		25 2 1 0 u
26		26 2 1 0 u
27		27 2 1 0 u
28		28 2 1 0 u
29		29 2 1 0 u
30		30 2 1 0 u

denote Print Limited 0121 520 5100

Sample answer sheet: Reading and Use of English

CAMBRIDGE ENGLISH
Language Assessment
Part of the University of Cambridge

Do not write in this box

SAMPLE

Candidate Name
If not already printed, write name
in CAPITALS and complete the
Candidate No. grid (in pencil).

Candidate Signature

Examination Title

Centre

Supervisor:
If the candidate is ABSENT or has WITHDRAWN shade here

Centre No.

Candidate No.

Examination
Details

Candidate Answer Sheet

Instructions

Use a PENCIL (B or HB).
Rub out any answer you wish to change using an eraser.

Parts 1, 3 and **4:**
Mark ONE letter for each question.

For example, if you think **B** is the
right answer to the question, mark
your answer sheet like this:

Part 2:
Write your answer clearly in CAPITAL LETTERS.

Write one letter or number in each box.
If the answer has more than one word, leave one
box empty between words.

For example:

| 0 | A | N | | E | X | A | M | P | L | E | | | |

Turn this sheet over to start.

CAE L

DP803

© UCLES 2014 Photocopiable

159

Sample answer sheet: Listening

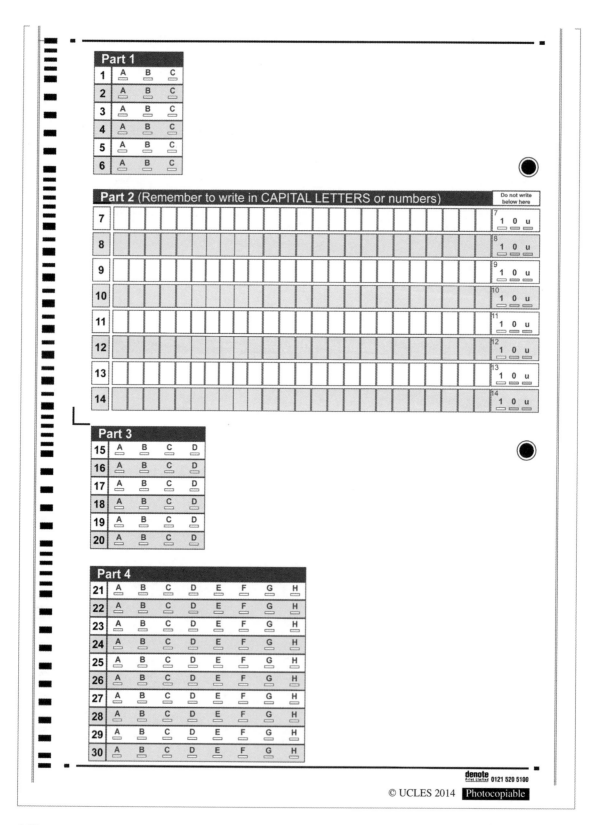

160

Thanks and acknowledgements

The authors and publishers acknowledge the following sources of copyright material and are grateful for the permissions granted. While every effort has been made, it has not always been possible to identify the sources of all the material used, or to trace all copyright holders. If any omissions are brought to our notice, we will be happy to include the appropriate acknowledgements on reprinting.

Text acknowledgements

Guardian News & Media Ltd for the text on p. 8 adapted from 'The Camera Always Lies' by Jonathan Jones, *The Guardian*, 29.8.2012. Copyright © Guardian News & Media Ltd; Guardian News & Media Ltd for the text on p. 10 adapted from 'Online passwords – what everyone should know' by Oliver Burkeman, *The Guardian*, 29.8.2012. Copyright © Guardian News & Media Ltd; Time Warner for the text on p. 14 adapted from 'Biography of Jean Piaget' from *People of the Century, 1999*. Copyright © 1999 by Time Magazine; International Debate Education Association for the text on p. 16 adapted from 'This House Believes that advertising is harmful' by the International Debate Education Association. Copyright © 2005 International Debate Education Association. All rights reserved; Geographical Magazine Limited for the text on p. 18 adapted from 'Secrets of the Deep' by Jonathan Green, *Geographical Magazine*, October 2012. Copyright © Geographical Magazine Limited; Guardian News & Media Ltd for the text on p. 21 adapted from 'The Rise of Home Working' by Phil Daoust, *The Guardian*, 2.8.2010. Copyright © Guardian News & Media Ltd; Guardian News & Media Ltd for the text and listening on p. 25 adapted from 'This column will change your life; selfishness' by Oliver Burkeman, *The Guardian*, 19.10.2012. Copyright © Guardian News & Media Ltd; Australian Broadcasting Corporation for the text and listening on p. 27 adapted from 'What's Left to Explore' *Future Tense*, 26.2.2012. Copyright © 2012 by Australian Broadcasting Corporation; Deloitte Parasport for the text and listening on p. 28 adapted from various interviews on www.parasport.org. uk. Copyright © Deloitte Parasport; Telegraph Media Group for the text on p. 30 adapted from 'Promotion is good for the heart' by Stephen Adams, *The Telegraph*, 8.6.2012. Copyright © 2012 by The Telegraph Media Group; Macmillan Publishers for the text on p. 32 adapted and excerpted from *Missing Ink* by Philip Hensher. Copyright 2012 by Philip Hensher; Ashmolean Museum, University of Oxford for the text on p. 33 adapted from www.ashmolean.org. © Ashmolean Museum, University of Oxford; Penguin Book Group for the text on p. 36 adapted and excerpted from *Cleopatra's Sister* by Penelope Lively. Copyright © 1993 by Penelope Lively; Trinity News for the text on p. 38 adapted from 'Sports Psychology Worth the Attention' by Daragh McCashin, *Trinity News*, 11.2.2010. Copyright © Trinity News. All rights reserved; Financial Times Corporation for the text on p. 40 adapted from 'Safaris and stargazing in Tanzania' by Jonathan Ford, *The Financial Times*, 3.15.2013. Copyright © The Financial Times Corporation; New Scientist for the text on p. 43 adapted from 'In the Eye of the Beholder' by Kat Austen, *New Scientist*, July 2012. Copyright © 2012 Reed Business Information UK. All rights reserved. Distributed by Tribune Media Services; Laura Stack for the text and listening on p. 46 adapted from 'I'm going to be on time if it kills me' by Laura Stack, http:// theproductivitypro.com. Copyright © Laura Stack. Reproduced by permission; Australian Broadcasting Corporation for the text and listening on p. 49 adapted from 'The Information Bingers' *Future Tense*, 12.2.2012. Copyright © by Australian Broadcasting Corporation; The Telegraph Media Group for the text on p. 54 adapted from 'Gap Year Travel: Does Time Out Really Enrich?' by Tommy Cookson, *The Telegraph*, 10.8.2012. Copyright © The Telegraph Media Group; The Telegraph Media Group for the text on p. 55 adapted from 'A History of Hair: Dos and Don'ts' by Kate Finnigan, *The Telegraph*, 5.2.2011. Copyright © The Telegraph Media Group; Guardian News & Media Ltd for the text on p. 58 adapted from 'Meet 'Dr. Love,' the Scientist Exploring What Makes People Good or Evil' by Oliver Burkeman, 15.7.2012. Copyright © Guardian News & Media Ltd; Guardian News & Media Ltd for the text on p. 62 adapted from 'Before Google... the Alternative Travel Guide to Poland' by Vicky Baker, *The Observer*, 6.10.2012. Copyright © Guardian News & Media Ltd; Australian Broadcasting Corporation for the text and listening on p. 71 adapted from 'Cardboard, paper and play' *Future Tense*, 17.6.2012. Copyright © by Australian Broadcasting Corporation; The Evening Standard for the text and listening on p. 72 adapted from 'Meet the Slashers' by Hannah Nathanson, *Evening Standard*, 7.9.2012. Copyright © 2012 The Evening Standard. All rights reserved;

Guardian News & Media Ltd for the text on p. 76 adapted from 'How Technology is Helping People With Speech Impairments to Talk' by Jon Henley, *The Guardian*, 16.9.2012. Copyright © Guardian News & Media Ltd; Sydney Morning Herald for the text on p. 77 adapted from 'Eight-House Sleep Unnatural, Say Experts' by Luke Malone, *The Sydney Morning Herald*, 16.3.2012. Copyright © 2012 by Sydney Morning Herald; Guardian News & Media Ltd for the text on p. 87 adapted from 'So you want to work in… Archaeology' by Liz Ford, *The Guardian*, 15.12.2007. Copyright © Guardian News & Media Ltd; The Independent for the text on p. 87 adapted from 'Archaeology: It's Not Just About Digging' by Kate Hilpern, *The Independent*, 11.9.2006. Copyright © The Independent; WAMU for the text and listening on p. 90 adapted from 'E-Books and Libraries' *The Diane Rehm Show*, 28.8.2012. Copyright © WAMU; Guardian News & Media Ltd for the text and listening on p. 92 adapted from 'Mars Mission' by Roman Charles, *The Guardian*, 25.2.2012. Copyright © Guardian News & Media Ltd; Bob Books for the text and listening on p. 93 adapted from 'Interview: Wildlife Photographer of the Year 2011 Daniel Beltrá' *Bob Books*, 23.11.2011. Copyright © Bob Books.

Photo acknowledgements

Key: T = Top, C = Centre, B = Below.

p. C1 (T): Alamy/©Ilkka Uusitalo – climbing; p. C1 (B): Corbis/Aurora Open/©Krystle Wright; p. C1 (C): Corbis/©Mike Zens; p. C2 (T): Corbis/Kalish/©DiMaggio; p. C2 (C): Alamy/©Oote Boe Photography; p. C2 (B): Alamy/©Image Source; p. C4 (T): Corbis/SuperStock/©Purestock; p. C4 (C): CorbisBlend Images/©Hill Street Studios; p. C4 (B): Corbis/©David Madison; p. C5 (T): Corbis/Blend Images/©Hill Street Studios; p. C5 (C): Shutterstock/Pressmaster; p. C5 (B): Corbis/ZUMA Press/©Chris Szagola; p. C7 (T): Corbis/©Ocean; p. C7 (C): Corbis/©Jenny Elia Pfeiffer; p. C7 (B): Corbis/Blend Images/©Peter Dressel; p. C8 (T): Alamy/©Steve Vidler; p. C8 (C): Alamy/©travelib asia; p. C8 (B): Alamy/©Ingram Publishing; p. C10 (T): Corbis/First Light/©Haiku Expressed; p. C10 (C): Corbis/©Tetra Images; p. C10 (B): Corbis/Blend Images/©ERproductions Ltd; p. C11 (T): Thinkstock/Digital Vision/Ryan McVay; p. C11 (C): Alamy/©i stagep; C11 (B): FremantleMedia International.

Visual materials for the Speaking test

- Why have these sports become popular?
- What motivates people to take them up?

- Why might the people be making calls in these places?
- How difficult might the calls be to make?

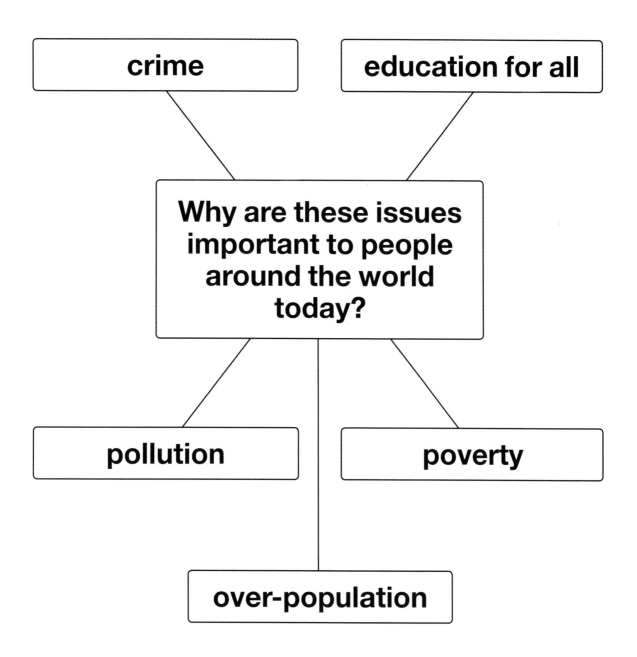

Visual materials for the Speaking test

- Why might people have chosen to experience these things?
- How might they be feeling?

- Why might people be having these discussions?
- What might the results of their discussions be?

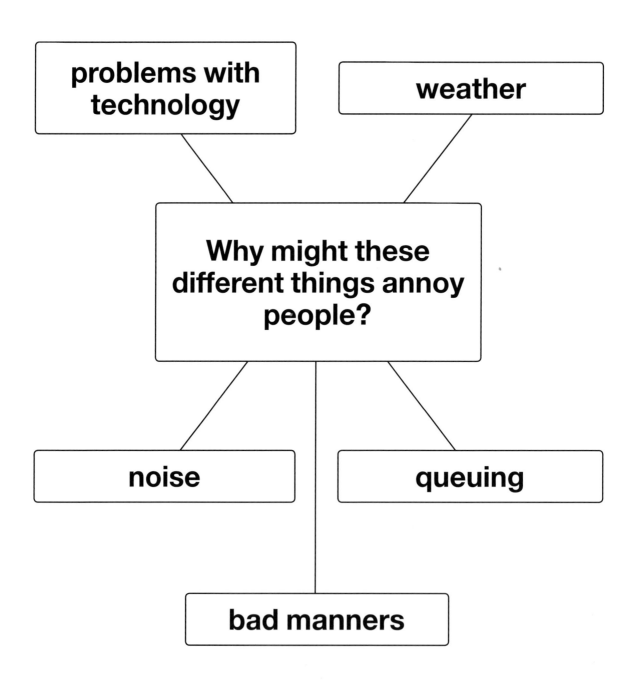

- How important is it to be creative in these different situations?
- How difficult might this be?

Visual materials for the Speaking test

- Why might the people enjoy working in these different places?
- What difficulties might they have?

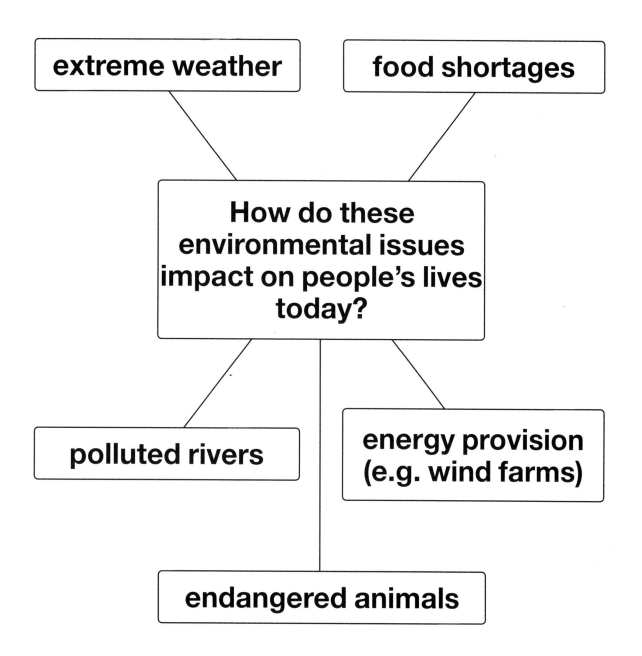

- How important is it to be careful in these different situations?
- What might happen if they made a mistake?

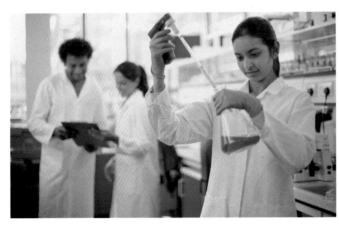

- Why might the people have entered these competitions?
- How might they be feeling?

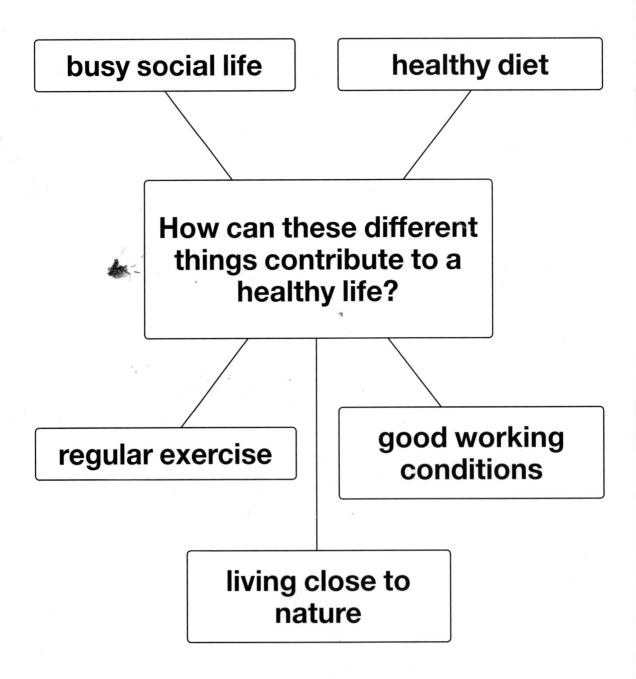

busy social life

healthy diet

How can these different things contribute to a healthy life?

regular exercise

good working conditions

living close to nature